Collins *practical gardener*

PLANTS FOR
SHADE

Collins practical gardener

PLANTS FOR SHADE

PHILIP CLAYTON

First published in 2005 by HarperCollins*Publishers*

77–85 Fulham Palace Road, London, W6 8JB

The Collins website address is:

www.collins.co.uk

Text by Phil Clayton; copyright © HarperCollins*Publishers*

Artworks and design © HarperCollins*Publishers*

The majority of photographs in this book were taken by
Tim Sandall. A number of other images were supplied
by David Sarton

Cover photography by Tim Sandall

Photographic props: Coolings Nurseries, Rushmore Hill,
Knockholt, Kent, TN14 7NN, www.coolings.co.uk

Design and editorial: Focus Publishing, Sevenoaks, Kent

Project editor: Guy Croton

Editor: Vanessa Townsend

Project co-ordinator: Caroline Watson

Design & illustration: David Etherington

Editorial assistants: Katie Lovell and George Croton

For HarperCollins

Senior managing editor: Angela Newton

Editor: Alastair Laing

Assistant editor: Lisa John

Design manager: Luke Griffin

Production: Chris Gurney

Contents

Introduction

Shade is a phenomenon common to all gardens. Even the sunniest, hottest gardens have areas where for at least part of the day, shade is cast by trees, buildings or other structures. In hot regions of the world, such as the Mediterranean and the Middle East, shade is a desirable factor, as it offers a cooling retreat from the relentless rays of the sun. Gardens in these hotter climes have historically tended to be placed in courtyards with high boundary walls shading at least part of the garden, and may feature spreading 'shade' trees or man-made structures such as vine-clad pergolas specifically to provide an escape from the heat. By contrast, in cooler regions, shade is more often seen as a problem, especially during dreary temperate winters.

Regardless of where you garden, try to see shade as an asset, that if treated correctly will enhance the qualities of a garden, broadening both its aesthetic appeal and the range of plants which can be grown and enjoyed within it. As modern gardens decrease in size, squeezed in between tall buildings, or hemmed in by high fences, shade is likely to become ever more commonplace. Some gardens in these situations may receive little if any direct sunlight at all, so light that is available must be maximized and various visual and horticultural tricks employed to brighten the area.

When planting your garden, you must choose carefully. There is little point struggling with sickly-looking sun-loving plants such as Cistus (sunrose) and Lavandula (lavender) in shade when you could be enjoying the luxuriance of lush ferns and other foliage plants that will thrive in these conditions. This does not mean that flowering species have no place in shade – many do; it is just a matter of selecting the appropriate kinds. It is also important to consider the use of plants with coloured leaves in shade. Golden or variegated foliage provides long-lasting bright colour and can be used to fine effect in shady areas; indeed, many plants with such foliage suffer in sunlight, the delicate leaves burning easily.

You will find many shade-loving plants almost maintenance-free and easy to grow if they are properly planted and cared for from the outset. Shady areas tend to be fairly sheltered and have higher humidity levels than those in full sun. This means that plants are exposed to less air movement, which combined with increased humidity levels helps cut down on watering requirements. The shelter also results in plants having some protection from the coldest winter weather.

It is true that in exceptional circumstances of deepest, driest shade, finding plants that will thrive is almost impossible. In these areas, you may find that using plants in containers, sculptures or hard landscaping alternatives can provide an effective solution.

Treat it properly and a shady garden can serve as a charming, sheltered retreat from hot summer sun or freezing winter winds. Areas of shade in the larger garden offer contrasting conditions that may be enhanced to provide homes for plants that would not thrive elsewhere, giving a different feel and increasing diversity throughout the outside rooms of your home.

All gardens have shady areas; the thing is to make the most of them with imaginative plantings

How to Use This Book

This book is divided into three parts. The opening chapter introduces you to types of plants that will flourish in a shady garden, how to manage shady areas, creative design solutions, good planting combinations, ideas to add colour and lift a dark, gloomy corner and finally, general care and maintenance of your garden and plants. A comprehensive plant directory follows, with individual entries on over 130 of the most commonly available plants for shade. These are listed in alphabetical order. The final section of the book covers particular plant problems. Troubleshooting pages allow you to diagnose the likely cause of any problems, and a directory of pests and diseases offers advice on how to solve them.

latin name of the plant genus, followed by its **common name**

detailed descriptions give specific advice on care for each plant, including pruning and pests and diseases

alphabetical tabs on the side of the page, colour-coded to help you quickly find the plant you want

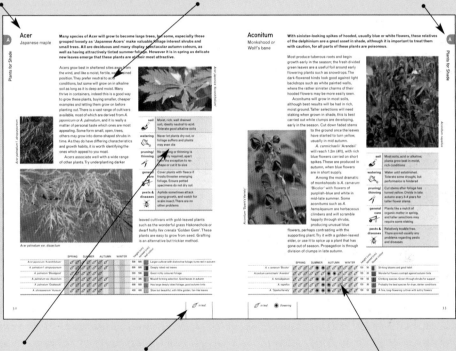

care charts provide an at-a-glance summary of the plant's specific needs (N.B. Where more than one genus appear on the page, the chart may cater for both plants)

a key at the bottom of the page explains what each symbol means

variety charts list recommended varieties for most genera of conservatory and greenhouse plants that feature more than one variety. These display key information to help you choose your ideal plant, showing:

• when (or if) the plant is in flower during the year
• when (or if) the plant is in leaf during the year
• the height and spread after optimum growth
• the principal colour of the flowers (or foliage)
• additional comments from the author

Assessing Your Garden for Shade

Most parts of your garden will receive some shade at certain times of the day, but particular areas will be shaded for longer periods.

The most constant form of shade is that cast by buildings and evergreen. If your garden is surrounded on several sides, the sun will be blocked out except when it is directly overhead. Some areas will never receive direct sunlight. Even so, a considerable amount of light will reach the ground. Fortunately, there are lots of attractive plants which will thrive in this situation. Indeed, there is great potential in this kind of shade. Similar conditions may be found in narrow areas, perhaps between a fence and the house. This sort of site is typically found in small town gardens, where the entire plot may be affected, or in limited areas of larger plots.

You may well have shady walls or fences in or forming the boundary to your garden, but unless overshadowed by other structures, the shade here is lighter and simpler to deal with. These areas may suffer from a rain-shadow effect; rainfall deflected away from the base of the wall or fence means the ground will be dry, and any plants sited here will need extra water, at least while establishing.

If your garden is filled with many mature trees or large shrubs it will also experience shade. It may be dappled (where the sunlight is lightly filtered) around the edge of

KEY

The yellow line denotes sunshine in the garden. On one side the sun will shine in the morning, on the other, in the afternoon.

This blue arrow denotes the direction of wind. In this case, the wind swirls over the fence and across the border beneath.

This green arrow denotes a gradient in the garden floor. In this case, the garden slopes from one end to another.

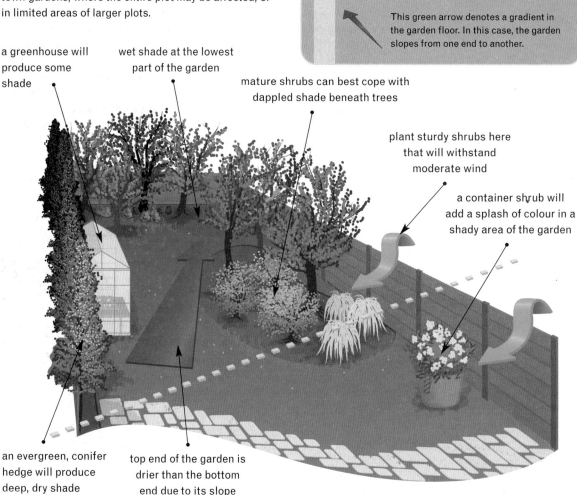

a greenhouse will produce some shade

wet shade at the lowest part of the garden

mature shrubs can best cope with dappled shade beneath trees

plant sturdy shrubs here that will withstand moderate wind

a container shrub will add a splash of colour in a shady area of the garden

an evergreen, conifer hedge will produce deep, dry shade

top end of the garden is drier than the bottom end due to its slope the wooded area or if the canopy is broken. However, under a dense canopy the shade may be quite deep. Dappled shade is a situation only possible under living plants, with leaves constantly moving in the breeze and light concentrations fluctuating. Deciduous trees cast substantial shade during the growing season, but let light through in winter and early spring. This characteristic is capitalized on by many plants found in woodlands which start growth early in the season, before tree leaves begin to grow, and it is these same plants (or selections from them) which may be used in the shady garden.

Shade is likely to be particularly intense under evergreen trees, as they have the densest canopies. Few species will thrive in these conditions, such as in plantations of coniferous trees, where other plants rarely survive beneath. However, few gardens are filled with large conifers to the same extent. If you feel that you have too many, the best solution may be selective thinning.

If you are planning changes to planting, or if re-designing your garden, it is a good idea to examine where shade falls, what kind of shade it is, and what part of the day it occurs in. this is best done over the course of a year as the shade may alter through the changing seasons.

In which direction does your garden face?

It is quite simple to get an idea of the orientation of your garden by observing which parts receive the most sun, but to be more precise, use a compass to see if you are likely to have a generally sunny or shady garden. In the northern hemisphere, gardens facing south receive the most sun during the day, are quick to warm up in spring and are more likely to suffer in hot summers. If your garden faces north, you will only receive limited sunlight in summer, perhaps in early morning and at the end of the day. Temperatures in north-facing gardens will be lower and in winter the site will be shaded; however, these conditions will suit many shade loving plants. Gardens that face east or west have a more balanced amount of sunlight and do not experience extremes in temperature. Such conditions allow a wide range of plants to be grown. West-facing gardens receive sun in the afternoon, east-facing in the morning, which may damage some plants such as camellias in winter. These are rather sensitive after a night frost. In the southern hemisphere, conditions are reversed, and the ideal aspect for maximum sun levels is north-east facing. Once you have worked out which way your garden faces, consider local factors such as trees and buildings, which will also cast shade.

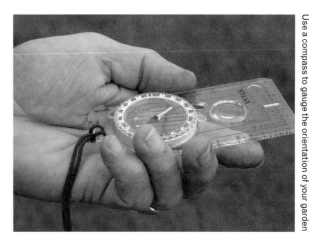

Use a compass to gauge the orientation of your garden

Where does the shade fall?

Over the course of a year, observe where the shady areas and where the sunny parts of your garden lie. Draw a sketch of the garden and note this down. On your plan, give some indication of what time of day the shade falls and for how long. In winter some areas may receive no direct sunlight, the sun perhaps being obscured by a pergola or a shed.

Your 'garden shade plan' can then form the basis to any planting that is subsequently carried out. Remember that as your garden becomes established the areas where shade falls will alter and are likely to increase as trees and shrubs mature, hedges grow and thicken, and new structures such as glasshouses are erected.

Some areas may be in permanent shade, others only at certain times of the day

Importance of soil type

It is useful at this stage to examine your garden soil, as this will have an effect on the conditions and play a part in determining what you can plant.

If the soil is heavy to dig, forming large clods and feels sticky to touch, you are likely to have a clay soil. In shade, a clay soil is likely to provide dry shade in summer and wet shade in winter. This will be awkward to cultivate and is best opened up with grit and organic matter to improve drainage. Sandy soils are light to work and feel gritty to touch, and may become almost dust-like in dry periods. In shade, they need improving with moisture-retaining organic matter to allow shade-loving plants to flourish. Silty soil is usually dark in colour and feels smooth to touch. It is usually easily worked and rich in organic matter and less prone to either drying out or waterlogging.

Dry, moist or wet shade?

In your garden you are likely to come across the following types of shade:

Dry shade Shaded areas by trees, hedges or shrubs often have the added problem of a dry, rooty, often nutrient-starved soil that makes establishing new plants difficult. The ground is sponge-like, with any rain that falls soon soaked up by networks of plant roots. The soil itself is consequently impoverished and may even become dust-like. This condition is one that many gardeners find a challenge and indeed it can be difficult to overcome. The solution is to try to improve soil conditions beneath, and to choose plants naturally adapted to similar conditions in the wild.

A sandy soil will exacerbate the dry conditions, as in the summer, as will a clay soil, so it is essential to add organic matter such as well-rotted manure to increase the amount of moisture the soil can hold. Look for this kind of shade beneath overhanging structures, mature plantings and by walls and fences, where rainfall is intercepted before it reaches the ground, while below the surface, roots of established trees and shrubs fill the soil, turning it into a virtual sponge.

Plants that survive well in these conditions tend to come from woodland situations and have glossy evergreen foliage that absorbs maximum light in gloomy conditions, yet does not lose too much moisture. These include *Pachysandra terminalis*, *Euphorbia amygdaloides* var. *robbiae*, ivies, some ferns, *Buxus sempervirens* (box) and *Iris foetidissima*. Certain bulbous plants may also do well as they are adapted to dry soils, holding moisture in their specially developed storage organs – that is, bulbs, tubers, rhizomes or corms.

Moist shade Most gardeners would perhaps describe this as the ideal kind of shade for growing the widest possible range of plants. It is no surprise that this shade is similar to conditions found in deciduous woodlands and forests where the ground is usually rich with organic matter, fallen leaves and general detritus from the trees above that enriches and retains soil moisture.

TESTING SOIL pH

It is essential before planting to determine the pH of your garden soil (that is, whether it is acidic or alkaline). In the natural woodland habitats where shade-loving plants flourish, fallen leaves and other organic materials accumulate over the years, creating a moisture-retentive, humus-rich soil which is naturally acidic, even if the underlying soil is alkaline. This is an important consideration when choosing shade-loving plants for the garden, as many woodland plants grow best in acidic soil. Checking for pH can be easily done using a special test kit available from garden centres. If your soil is acidic (having a low pH), then you will be able to suit the needs of almost all woodland plants. On an alkaline (high pH) soil you will have some restrictions. Plants such as rhododendrons, Pieris, camellias and some lilies will not survive in alkaline soil, and must be grown in pots of ericaceous (acidic) compost. However, there are many superb plants that will thrive on alkaline soil, including Berberis, Cyclamen, Mahonia, bamboos and most ferns.

If you have a neutral soil (neither acid nor alkaline, pH7) it is possible that over time you will eventually be able to grow some acid-loving species of plant, as long as the soil is built up and regularly improved with garden compost, well-rotted manure or leaf mould.

A well-stocked garden contains a mixture of plants for sun and shade

The only downside is that in particularly dry, hot conditions, the trees and shrubs remove greater amounts of moisture from the ground than usual and lower-growing, more delicate species can suffer.

If you have a moisture retaining soil, rich in organic matter, with a light canopy of deciduous trees, or perhaps a border by a shady wall or fence, this is the shade you will experience.

There are many wonderful woodland plants that thrive in these conditions. Many are at their most attractive in spring and early summer before tree canopies fully develop, although with careful selection year-round interest is possible, and should be aimed for. The range of suitable species from forests and woodlands from around the world is huge and includes hellebores, Trillium, many bamboos, some lilies, hydrangeas, geraniums, Heuchera, hostas, Epimedium – the list is almost endless.

Wet shade Areas that are wet and in shade are often thought of as dank and even stagnant. Ponds and pools here are seldom a success, as little will grow in them and they become filled with fallen leaves and debris unless carefully maintained. In constantly wet soil there are species of plant that thrive and may assist in drying it out a little. The key is to maximize light and to improve soil drainage.

Look for this situation in the lowest lying areas of the garden where water naturally collects, or by areas where runoff from sheds and out-buildings collects. If you have a soggy clay soil, this situation is made more likely.

Plants that will grow well here, as long as the ground is not constantly waterlogged, include some ferns, hostas, Rodgersia, primulas, some species of Cornus (dogwood).

SHADE IN NATURAL HABITATS

When you come to select plants for the garden it is useful to understand the habitats from which many of the plants originally come from, as this can assist when caring for them. Wild habitats may also give clues to successful planting partners and combinations.

Different natural habitats have developed their own plant communities, where over time species have evolved to be well-adapted to fill their own particular niches or roles within the community. Most shade-loving plants come from the world's many temperate woodlands and forests which are usually composed of several distinct layers. At the top of the community will be the large dominant tree or trees, such as the oak or beech, followed by shrubs including holly, honeysuckle and elder. In the bottom layer, growing in the shade beneath these are the smaller non-woody or herbaceous plants such as primulas, bluebells and ferns. When planting a garden from scratch it should be remembered that this naturally tiered pattern of growth is the scenario into which many plants will most comfortably fit.

Examine the current planting

Once you have assessed your garden for shade, take a look at what is already growing. Plants that are obviously thriving will be in the correct positions, while those shy to bloom might need more sun. Others may show signs of receiving too much sun with scotched foliage, or may simply wilt through lack of water and excessive heat. These plants should be moved to more suitable areas. Some traditional garden features may be inappropriate. For example, a lawn in deep shade makes little sense as the grass soon dies and the area becomes overrun with moss. Hard landscaping alternatives (for example, paving) will be far more successful and easy to maintain.

Managing shade

As a garden matures the conditions begin to alter and it is important that planting and the design of the garden adapts to cater for these changes. For example, areas under maturing shrubs and trees can start to be planted with shade loving plants once the lower branches are removed, allowing light in underneath, and increasing the number of plants which may be cultivated (see p16).

Removing individual branches to let the rain in, and adding organic matter to raise the depth of the soil, may be effective measures to allow new plants to become established beneath.

You may decide that some parts of the garden are to remain in full sun, so in these areas, overhanging tree branches or the over-enthusiastic growth of shrubs may

Prune some shrubs each year to maintain light levels

have to be reduced to allow the sun's rays to pass unhindered. In a densely planted garden, a careful autumn or winter prune should become an annual event to prevent the entire garden becoming one of shade (see p29). Reducing the height of hedges also has dramatic effects in the garden, especially in winter, allowing the sloping sunlight access to previously dark corners (see p17). It can be quite surprising how quickly a once-sunny area can become dappled shade. The growth of sun-loving plants is curtailed by shade so it is important to let the sun back in as soon as possible.

A shady area can be relieved by a feature, such as this Cordyline

The best combinations of shade loving plants feature strong contrasts in colour and form

When you are planning your planting, bear in mind that a garden should not be static, and if areas have to be changed to adapt to changing conditions after several years this should not be seen as a failure but as an opportunity to grow a wider range of different plants.

Creating shade

You may decide that your garden is too sunny. Perhaps there is little planting and few structures, and the area feels too open and exposed. Shade is easily created in a small garden by planting a deciduous tree. The shade it will eventually provide can then be planted up. Alternatively plant several small trees and create a little glade with associated woodland planting beneath. A group of large shrubs on the boundary will also prevent the garden feeling too open and cast shade, if you feel that the area is too small for a tree. A border created in front of these shrubs will in turn provide cooler, darker conditions.

As an alternative, construct a pergola or arbour, and plant with climbers. These will scramble up the supports and over the top, casting shade beneath.

TIP
If your garden is long and narrow, it can be divided up with screens or trellis, and planted with climbers. A small border could be created behind and filled with shade-loving species, or you could build a wide pergola, with space for planting pockets beneath.

ADVANTAGES & DISADVANTAGES OF SHADE

Advantages
- protection from summer heat – ideal for sitting out; less watering required
- increased shelter from winds
- reduced weed growth – many weeds need sun to thrive and spread
- some frost protection – tree canopies mean evening temperatures are higher
- wide range of plants may be cultivated – with protection from drying wind, summer sun and winter chill, a greater range of plants will grow

Disadvantages
- plants that require full sun will fail – many require summer heat to ripen wood that produces flowers
- lawns tricky to keep – especially in heavier shade, it is better to do away with lawns altogether
- falling leaves in autumn – shade cast by deciduous trees will be followed by autumn leaf fall that must be cleared
- new plants difficult to establish – soil near walls or next to trees and shrubs is likely to suffer from drought

Any interesting garden will be a harmonious blend of good, strong design and effective planting. In gardens of deep shade, the design will be shaped in part by the need to maximize light, whereas in gardens with both shady and sunny areas, the design may enhance conditions to provide a contrasting feel between the different parts.

When you are planning your planting design remember that good initial selection of plants and appropriate planting densities are most important if the entire garden is not to become one of shade. Your aim should be to plant up areas to mature in around five years. This should result in an easily-maintained garden where plants have plenty of room to grow. Gaps may be filled with shade tolerant bulbs and annuals. In some areas you may desire only light shade, while elsewhere, deeper shade may be acceptable and planting densities can be tighter.

Design Solutions in Shade

While it is usually impossible (without drastic action) to transform a shady garden into a sunny one, there are certain tricks and techniques you can use when designing or re-designing a garden to maximize the available light and overcome other problems symptomatic of shade. Shaded gardens often have great potential, but are all too often abandoned by owners after new but inappropriate plants fail.

Painted walls and the use of trellis

If your garden is overshadowed by walls and high fences, extra light will be received if these surfaces are painted white, or a light-reflecting colour, bouncing sunlight back around the garden. Saturated (dark) colours absorb light and make an area seem much gloomier. Alternatively, decorative trellis can be painted white and attached to walls. Trellis is easily available and today comes in a wide range of designs and types, some of the more ornamental has smaller-sized spaces (that is, more woodwork) and may be formed in to rounded panels or other shapes. This in turn can be clothed with a shade-tolerant climbers such as Lonicera

(honeysuckle) or Akebia (chocolate vine), but it may be best to prevent the plant covering all the trellis, or the light-reflecting qualities will be lost.

Mirrors

Using mirrors in the garden is no longer the preserve of those who design for the Chelsea Flower Show. As well as bouncing light back into the garden they can help a small space appear larger – especially useful in a city garden or courtyard. With mirrors it is all about placement. Put one in too prominent or obvious a location and the whole effect will appear contrived; the trick is also revealed too soon for it to succeed. Better to place it out of the main line of vision, perhaps at an angle, and to partially obscure it, ideally with vegetation. This will then fool the uninitiated into thinking there is another secluded section of the garden waiting to be discovered!

Avoid placing mirrors where the sun can bounce directly off them, which again gives the game away, but then this is not likely to be a problem in shade!

The best mirrors to use outside are made of mirrored stainless steel, as they are the most durable. These are probably best battened onto the wall, or attached with an adhesive resin.

Raised beds

A common complaint of those who garden in dry shade is that nothing will establish in the thin, impoverished rooty soil beneath existing planting. While gradual soil improvement will eventually help, the quickest route to success is to create raised beds where the soil level is lifted significantly above all the existing troublesome roots and dusty earth. Even beds raised by around 30cm (12in) will provide enough additional depth of soil for many lower growing plants, even some of the smaller shrubs. Railway sleepers are ideal for this, but consider logs, loose bricks and even wooden boards retained with pegs. You would be better to avoid log roll or plastic edging materials, as these look too artificial and rarely prove durable. Larger-growing plants will require greater soil depth, where beds need decent, purpose-built retaining walls built of bricks, stone (both of which may require

The reflective qualities of a wall painted white can really brighten a shady corner

footings) or stacked railway sleepers. Remember to allow plenty of seep holes (holes in the sides of the walls for drainage) which can either be incorporated between bricks at the time of construction or drilled through the mortar later. Also, fill the bottom third of the bed with additional drainage material such as builder's rubble,

stones or even polystyrene. Failure to do this will result in soil becoming waterlogged and plants rotting-off.

Raised beds have certain advantages. They allow a range of ericaceous or acid soil-loving plants to be cultivated in areas where the underlying soil is alkaline, so long as the bed is filled with a suitably acidic soil. Raised beds are likely to be well drained (provided the seep holes and additional drainage have been incorporated) – an important property, especially if some of the plants are of borderline hardiness. Another advantage is ease of maintenance; bending is minimized when weeding, as it is possible to sit on the edges of the bed rather than stoop or kneel on the ground.

Pay heed to existing trees when raising soil level. Never be tempted to significantly lift soil levels directly around the trunk of a tree, as this will kill it.

Planting in pots and containers

Perhaps the simplest and easiest way to introduce colour and interest into areas of deep shade is to use plants in pots and containers. There are many advantages to this method.

The plants will grow in a reservoir of compost, therefore the quality of the garden soil is unimportant and, as with raised beds, plants requiring acidic soil can be easily cultivated. Plants in pots are easily fed and watered and can be moved around and grouped in different ways, creating an ever-changing focal point.

Any plants that are starting to look tired or are out of flower can be moved from sight and replaced with others. Plants that need more sun are quite happy to spend short spells in shade, and can be returned to brighter areas if they begin to suffer.

If your garden is entirely paved, with no open ground, potted plants are the only easy option. Line the pots with crocks to ensure good drainage [A]. Larger containers can be planted with several different plants [B], whereas smaller ones will be best with a single specimen. Water all plants in thoroughly, as soon as you have planted them in the pots [C].

When you are grouping plants together, remember that the rules of form (general shape), texture (the general effect of foliage) and colour (be it flowers and/or foliage) are as relevant here as when planting into the open ground, so arrange the plants with care, ensuring that they sit comfortably together [D].

As a general rule, it is best to put the larger plants at the back of the group where they will serve as a foil. Try to contrast plant shapes, for instance offsetting spiky plants with rounded ones. Sometimes a plant may be too low for the display; this problem is easily dealt with by elevating the plant on an upturned pot. If the group is in the middle of an area and will be viewed from several angles, the largest plant is best placed centrally, with lower ones around it. Groups of plants are often most effective in corners, softening hard surfaces and filling unused space.

You may decide to colour theme the group, matching or contrasting colours with other plants or containers, but remember that lighter colours will work best, although a splash of a richer hue will be dramatic.

A  B

C  D

Raising tree canopies

Trees and shrubs that cast shade can be easily tackled by the careful removal and reduction of over hanging limbs. Low branches prevent light reaching directly under the tree from the sides and their removal can open up new planting opportunities. This may also stimulate the tree to grow taller, producing branches higher up. These higher tree canopies may block sunlight from above but still allow it in from the sides. Lower branches are generally easier to remove; any which are too large or require climbing to reach are best tackled by a qualified tree surgeon.

You will be surprised how much difference the removal of a few branches can make to a tree. This pruning may be best carried out in autumn or winter when a clear view of any deciduous tree's structure is possible. Equally surprising is the amount of material that will need disposing of once pruning has taken place! Reducing the height of boundary hedges may have a similarly lightening effect, brightening the garden inside.

> **TIP**
>
> As well as being pruned in such a way as to raise the canopy of branches, some trees and shrubs can be pruned to produce exotic foliage. These are mainly large leafed species, such as Ailanthus and Paulownia, as well as most Eucalyptus.

How to remove a tree branch You should only remove tree branches that you feel confident you can manage. Any which are from a neighbour's tree or reach over the fence should be left until you have informed other parties involved of your intentions. This way disputes may be avoided. Never climb a tree to remove a branch and try to avoid using ladders propped up against the trunk. Use a freestanding step ladder and ensure that someone holds the base to keep it steady. Beware that a branch that looks reasonably manageable often turns out to be larger and heavier than you expect. It is best to leave any work requiring potentially lethal chain saws to the experts!

The best kind of saw to use is one that is specially designed for tree pruning; these saws are usually small, flexible, light and folding in design. It is vital to use a sharp blade. Begin by identifying the branch that you wish to remove. If it is large and heavy, you will need to reduce it, rather than attempting to cut it off in one go. Begin to make a small under-cut (cutting from underneath) about 30cm (12in) away from the trunk or

limb you are cutting the branch back to [A]. Only cut about one third of the way through the branch. Next, begin to cut from above about 3cm (1in) away (closer to the trunk) from the under cut, aiming to end up with a staggered cut [B]. Continue until the heavy part of the branch is removed, leaving the 30cm (12in) stump still attached – the branch should simply snap off without a tear. Now locate where you wish the final cut to be. It should not be flush with the trunk (or main limb), but just out from it where the branch begins to flare. This region is called the collar and will help the eventual wound heal properly. Make a small under cut to sever the bark, but this time you can cut from directly above, so long as you hold the end of the stump to ensure a clean cut [C]. Do not seal or paint the wound.

Large mature shrubs can be pruned to resemble trees, with bare lower stems.

Removing lower branches raises the canopy of a tree

Dealing with hedges

If you are planning to plant a hedge, you may wish to consider the effects it will have on light in the garden, especially in winter. A tall hedge may block evening or morning sunshine – especially if it is evergreen – depending on the garden's orientation. This may be a problem or a virtue. Morning sun in winter can damage frosted plants such as camellias, so planting some low bushes or a hedge may prove beneficial. Alternatively, you can alter the height in some sections of the hedge, or even leave gaps to allow light into the garden.

Deciduous hedges such as those of hawthorn (Crataegus) will allow light through in winter and early spring, and thus allow a wider range of plants such as spring-flowering bulbs to grow directly by them. Also decide on the eventual height of the hedge. You don't want it to be too tall for ease of maintenance sake, and obviously the taller it is, the longer the shadows it will cast. To be sensible, a maximum height of 2.5m (8ft) is usually appropriate.

How to trim a hedge All the sides of the hedge will need to be trimmed, but the top will grow the quickest. To ensure the top of the hedge is level, string a line between two canes [A]. Spend a little time ensuring that it is level before you begin cutting the hedge along it. Lay a sheet on the ground to collect the clippings [B]. Trim the top of the hedge to the line, using hedge trimmers or shears [C]. If you cut regularly, shears are perfectly fine and will actually give the best finish, but for an annual prune (usually done in late summer or autumn), hedge trimmers will be far easier to use. Take care if using a step ladder.

The sides of the hedge are easier to cut and can usually be done by eye, but do check regularly for evenness of cut [D].

Most coniferous hedges must not be trimmed back too hard; avoid cutting into growth made more than one season ago. Serious height reduction on most conifer hedges will fail, leaving dead branches at the top. The hedge will never recover. Most deciduous hedges can be cut back much harder, as can yew (Taxus).

Use of hard landscaping materials

In some areas the amount of effort required to improve the soil for planting may be felt to outweigh the advantages and benefits that will be achieved.

A patio decorated with pots can save a lot of effort on poor soil

If your soil is so poor that it really is not worth digging it over and cultivating it, a fully-paved courtyard may suit you, with planting in containers. This way plants are easily controlled and looked after (even if they require much water during the summer months), and can be moved on if you decide to change house. Leaves can be easily swept up, and although stone, concrete and brick surfaces are particularly prone to a build-up of slippery, unsightly algae and moss, this is easily removed with a hose and power washer or with specially formulated chemicals if an area is very badly affected.

If you have an area with terrible dry rooty soil, try spreading gravel or slate chips on it over a permeable weed-suppressing membrane. Gravel is a useful material as it is cheap, non-slip, and is easily raked and replenished to keep fresh. Sculpture and ornamental pots of plants placed on top will create a tidy, attractive

A water butt conserves rainwater and is a useful resource in any garden

Tree circles

You may find dealing with areas under mature trees a problem, especially if the tree has a canopy reaching low to the ground. Light levels here are reduced and grass often grows poorly. Equally, mowing grass underneath is difficult and shallow-rooted trees may even be damaged. Certain species are liable to suckering and the woody stumps growing through the grass may damage the mower.

Mulching Some trees can have their canopies raised (see p16) and come to no harm, looking attractive with a clear trunk at the base. Other species such as cedars, Catalpa and magnolias lose their grace and appeal if the lower branches are cut off. If lower branches are retained, remove the turf to the drip line or outer edge of the canopy, and cover the soil with bark mulch. This gives a neat appearance, and a weed-suppressing membrane will not be required, as light is dim and weeds will be few and far between and easily removed. Simply cut edges and top up the mulch occasionally if it begins to degrade.

effect. Such an area may be themed and given perhaps a Japanese feel using potted bamboos in oriental containers, Japanese-style sculpture, and even a bamboo cane screen behind. However, gravel does prove a fiddle in autumn when clearing away leaves.

If you have a difficult area at the foot of an evergreen hedge – a notoriously difficult spot in the garden – why not try constructing a wood pile or stumpery, which both make ideal habitats for many species of insects and other animals. Many of these are beneficial: some, among them beetles and frogs, eat pests such as slugs and snails; other smaller ones, including ladybirds, will feed on aphids. Simply stack logs and branches (you can use those removed from trees in your own garden) into the area, and leave, although the pile may look more attractive planted with small ferns and ivy.

Alternatively, use the area for seating, as a storage area of the garden, or for placing sheds. The run-off of rainwater from the shed roof may then be used to keep a small section of the garden continuously moist, allowing associated plants to thrive. You could also add a water butt to save and hold rainwater. Choose one with a lid (to prevent birds and other animals drowning in it), and a tap at the base to allow easy removal of water. If the butt is positioned in shade, the water will not turn green and should be less prone to turning stagnant.

Mulch over tree circles to retain moisture

Naturalizing bulbs Other trees whose branches do not reach the ground may be treated differently. Where a tree is in a lawn, you may wish to retain the grass beneath, in which case any species of bulbs and other plants such as snowdrops (Galanthus), snowflakes (Leucojum), crocus, anemones, primulas, bluebells (Hyacinthoides) and daffodils (Narcissus) can be naturalized. After the attractive spring display is over, the grass is left to grow long, allowing bulb foliage to wither naturally. This enables the bulbs to store enough energy to flower well the following year. Avoid tying up the foliage – it looks ugly and reduces photosynthesis.

For early summer flowers, you could introduce camassias. These bulbs have long stalks that lift the blue or white flowers above the grass. Wild flowers may be allowed amid the longer grass, provided shade is light and dappled; this will create a relaxed and informal feel and will contrast with shorter grass away from the trees. Alternatively, grass can then be cut, and left short. You could add colchicums and autumn flowering crocus to continue the display late in the season, but be sure to mow off long grass before they appear.

When planting any of these bulbs, you should aim for a naturalistic effect. Simply scatter the bulbs and plant them where they fall, cutting trough the turf with an old kitchen knife and planting with a trowel. Alternatively you could use a special bulb planter.

Ground cover You may wish to use ground cover plants directly under a tree. Some such as ivy are particularly suitable and will grow in quite dense shade, suppressing weeds and providing a tidy evergreen carpet beneath. All that is required is an annual trim around the edge. Generally plants that creep across the ground like Vinca (periwinkle) or *Rubus tricolor* or those that sucker such as Pachysandra are best, but others with horizontal growth patterns such as prostrate junipers, *Lonicera pilata*, or even spectacular *Viburnum plicatum* 'Mariesii' will grow well. These can be planted 'en masse' or grouped to give a more varied show, although it is important not to provide too much competition for the tree. For this reason trees are best left plant-free underneath when young (one can have a few bulbs or annuals without harm). Many climbers including honeysuckle (Lonicera), *Hydrangea petiolaris* and even some roses can be placed close to the trunk in order to scramble up the tree. Some will do better planted midway between the trunk and drip line, and given a tall, stout cane reaching into the canopy to scramble up.

Planting a climber to grow up a tree If you are planting a climber such as *Schizophragma integrifolium* that clings to the trunk, dig a hole about 30cm (12in) from the base of the tree [A]. Otherwise, dig a hole further out, although well under the tree canopy. Improve the soil with organic matter and remove the plant from its pot. If the plant is self-clinging and to grow directly up the tree, remove any cane or support from the plant and place the plant in the hole, directing it towards the trunk [B]. Firm the plant and tie any stems that reach the tree flat against the trunk [C]. Water plants well [D] and mulch with well-rotted manure.

For scrambling climbers such as honeysuckle and rambling roses, position the plant and include a long cane that reaches to the canopy of the tree. Firm plant and tie any stems to it and remove some side shoots to encourage the climber to grow upwards. Eventually it will reach the canopy and grow away.

When planting, first mark out the circle, taking care to ensure it is even, with a hose, spray paint or a bottle filled with sand. Lift the turf by skimming it off with a spade, retaining as much topsoil as possible. Try to improve the soil by digging it over lightly with a fork. You will find thick roots that you should try not to damage; instead you are aiming to plant in pockets between them, where you may well find spongy, fibrous root which may be removed in small quantities. Add plenty of organic matter such as well-rotted manure, and perhaps mound the level of the soil slightly. Any odd low branches can be removed carefully. When planting remember that circular beds can be seen from all directions, so place taller plants closest to the trunk, smaller ones at the edge by the drip line.

Choosing Plants for Shade

What should you look for when choosing plants for a shady garden? Well, of course this all depends on the kind of shade you actually have and what the ground conditions are like, but there are a few general characteristics to look out for when picking suitable plants at the garden centre. These characteristics represent the physical adaptations the plants have evolved to survive in low-light situations. However, as in many walks of life, there are exceptions to these rules, and the best action is to consult a book or ask for advice where you see the plant offered.

Aucuba japonica has shiny, evergreen and variegated leaves

Leaves shiny and evergreen Many shrubs that grow in shade are evergreen (and greenish in colour, as opposed to silver) and have glossy, smooth, reflective leaves to maximize light uptake.
Examples include: *Aucuba japonica*, Buxus (box), camellias, *Fatsia japonica*, Ilex (hollies), and Hedera (ivies).

Leaves large and leathery Plants which produce large leaves usually do so to maximize the amount of light they can receive, as they would naturally grow in some shade. They are likely to originate from fairly moist areas, as water loss from large leaves is high.
Examples include: *Acanthus mollis*, Angelica, *Begonia grandis* subsp. *evansiana*, Bergenia, hellebores and Rodgersia.

Leaves soft and delicate Many woodland plants that revel in the high humidity often found in such conditions have soft, delicate foliage that is easily damaged by bright sunlight and desiccation. Examples include Asplenium, Chaerophyllum, Epimedium, Kierengeshoma and Matteuccia.

It is best to avoid plants with grey or silver leaves, or those with thick hair or woolly foliage. These characteristics are typical of plants from hot, sunny positions where plants need to reflect excessive light and retain any moisture. Similarly plants with narrow or needle-like leaves, aromatic foliage (including most herbs), or thick and waxy or succulent leaves are usually adaptations made by plants to survive in hot and sunny, often dry conditions. These too will fail in shade.

Matteuccia struthiopteris has soft, delicate leaves

Using colour from plants to brighten shade

Plants can play an invaluable role in the shaded garden by brightening up dark, gloomy corners with both foliage and flowers, making the garden seem larger and more appealing. Certain colours, especially bright yellows, lime-green, creams and of course white (not strictly a colour) reflect light making an area seem less dark, and providing an illuminating effect. Conversely, dark greens, blues and reds seem more light-absorbent and thus make little impact, if any, used in a low-light situation.

Use of foliage When you are choosing plants for shade, foliage colour is more important than flower colour as few plants for shade provide a spectacular, long-lasting floral display to rival those out in the sun. In shade the effects tend to be subtle and less strident. One way to bring colour into a shady area is to choose plants with attractively marked and coloured foliage. Plants that have leaves of more than one colour are known as 'variegated', where leaves are splashed, blotched, spotted centred or margined with cream, white, yellow, pink, red or varying shades of green. Alternatively, plants may have leaves of a single colour other than green, including blue, purple or yellow.

> **TIP**
> Be careful to avoid clashes of colour and decorative features in juxtaposed plants. Even in deep shade, if two plants 'overwhelm' one another by flowering in starkly contrasting colours at the same time, the desired effect could be ruined.

The bright foliage of *Choisya ternata* 'Sundance'

Most plants require some sun to bring out the brightest leaf colours, but others may be quite happy in shade, even if the colour is slightly reduced. In shade it is the brightest variegation and leaf colours which provide the most effective results, especially if it is yellow (often called gold), cream or white.

Some of these plants may actually be too vivid for widespread use in sun, their bright leaf colours clashing, and creating gaudy effects against the bright flowers of bedding plants. However, in shade they come into their own.

YEAR-ROUND APPEAL: SOIL

ACID SOIL
Even if you do not have acid soil, you can still grow many of these treasures in containers of ericaceous compost.

Winter
Hamamelis (witch hazels) – their spidery blooms survive the frostiest conditions.

Spring
Camellias – these offer marvellous colour in shades of pale pink, silvery-white and yellow.
Rhododendrons – for the most dazzling displays the deciduous types are unsurpassable.

Summer to Autumn
Himalayan poppies (Meconopsis), Eucryphia, Stewartia, Crinodendron – these continue the floral display until the first flames of autumn colour arrive as leaves begin to fall.

ALKALINE SOIL
Winter
Mahonia x *media* 'Charity' – scented yellow candles held above elegant evergreen foliage.
Jasminum nudiflorum – bare stems produce a multitude of golden trumpets.

Spring
Primulas, Bergenia (cerise, pink or white), sweetly-scented Convallaria (lily of the valley), nodding hellebores (white through to purple).
Clematis montana – a climber available in white and different hues of pink, with bulbs such as snowdrops (Galanthus), crocus and daffodils (Narcissus).

Summer
Digitalis (foxglove), geraniums, exotic-looking Hemerocallis, later-flowering hydrangeas.

Autumn
Cyclamen hederifolium – cheery pink and white flowers create a bright backdrop for autumn leaves.

jagged yellow leaves in spring, *Arum italicum* 'Marmoratum' has valuable white-splashed leaves which appear in the depths of winter, only to die down and helpfully create space in the spring. Among grasses, *Milium effusum* 'Aureum' is a desirable plant to have. It seeds freely around the garden producing clumps of golden and lime-green foliage that is most attractive in spring, creating a good foil for other woodland plants in flower.

Use of flowers Plants grown for flowers in shade can be used in combination with the foliage effects already described, or alternatively stand alone. If you are looking for flower colour in summer, a simple but most effective solution is simply to pot up containers of Impatiens (busy Lizzie). These plants are the best annual bedding for use in shade and can be removed from their pots and planted in the ground beneath other larger shrubs. They also thrive in hanging baskets. White or pale pink selections will be most effective and provide an excellent display from early summer until the first frosts, provided they are kept fed and watered. The best course with flowers is to use a predominance of light colours, and then provide effective contrasts with the darker, more saturated colours. These darker-coloured flowers can also be used in combination with the brighter foliage, as they will form an effective contrast and stand out. On their own they would be lost in the shade.

For golden foliage a classic choice is *Choisya ternata* 'Sundance', an evergreen shrub with brilliant yellow leaves and small white flowers in early summer. In sun this plant can be hideous, the leaves sometimes becoming bleached, but in shade the leaves are bright lime-green and can really lift a whole area. For huge leaves splashed with white, try a variegated *Fatsia japonica*, although this will need a sheltered garden. In colder areas, variegated hollies such as white-edged *Ilex* 'Silver Queen', or green and cream *Euonymus japonicus* 'President Gauthier' take on the same role. Smaller evergreens with coloured leaves such as *Ilex crenata* 'Golden Gem', variegated box (Buxus) and the many Euonymus with variegated foliage can be used to add a splash of colour under larger plants. Not all variegated and coloured leaf plants are evergreen. Sumptuous *Acer shirasawanum* 'Aureum' with golden leaves like little Chinese paper fans is magnificent; for a quick-growing alternative try *Cornus alba* 'Aurea', which has the bonus of colourful winter stems.

Some non-woody plants also have coloured foliage. *Acanthus mollis* 'Hollard's Gold' is a large plant with

Planting combinations in shade

Creating good planting combinations can be a long and complicated process, but in reality there are few hard and fast rules. However, there are some general guidelines which if followed usually result in an effective planting design. Plants have three main aesthetic characteristics:

Form This relates to the general shape of the plant – is it upright, spreading, spiky or mounded, and so on? In general it is best to create interest by combining plants of different forms, as this helps to emphasize their different shapes. You may combine low-growing bergenias with the upright, pointed form of *Iris foetidissima*, or perhaps add in the fountain-like shape of *Liriope muscari*. You may prefer to use a shrubby plant – possibly a twiggy cornus with coloured stems.

Texture The general effect of foliage (or sometimes branches and trunks) creates the textural quality. A plant with glossy leaves will seem shiny, whereas one with rough leaves looks matt. Some plants have hairy or downy leaves, giving them a soft appearance. Others may be bristly or feathery.

A gain, here you may wish to create contrasts in texture to add drama to a scene. For example, with leathery bergenias, you could contrast the delicate-looking fern, *Matteuccia struthiopteris*.

Colour This is the easiest feature to explain, but don't only think of the foliage or flowers in isolation, think of the two combined. A plant may have attractive golden leaves, but do you really want the candy floss-pink flowers it produces later to go with it? Also remember the stem and bark colour, if the plant is deciduous. Consider the use of variegated foliage to add colour

Low-growing plants combined with tall upright plants contrast well together

TIP

When combining plants in any situation, try to keep a general overview of how you want things to look rather than becoming overly focussed on one particular feature. The garden is a broad canvas of which your shady areas are just a part.

especially in shade where flower power is reduced. Overdo it though, and the effect is too busy and overwhelming. Colour is the characteristic most people think of. The simplest kind of colour scheme is to use hues that blend harmoniously together such as whites and yellows or pinks and purples, but greater drama is produced using contrasting but complimentary colours such as mixing yellow and blue or orange and purple. This can be taken further by adding vibrant touches of clashing colour, although great care should be taken when creating these effects. It is important especially in shade that green is remembered as a colour, and as we have already said, in these conditions it is yellows, white and pale colours which will lend the greatest impact.

What makes a satisfying planting combination is really all up to you. The best way to go about planting is perhaps to draw up a list of plants you wish to include in a particular area, chosen from this book or a nursery. It may be simplest to work from the larger plants down, establishing a framework that can then be added to with

Subtle shades of green and strong textures

other suitable smaller plants. As well as taking into account the above qualities, the more practical considerations must be addressed.

- Have you selected plants that will provide interest throughout the year?
- Are the plants of similar vigour? If you are mixing plants, perhaps growing one through another, this will be important.
- Is the eventual size of the plants suitable for the garden? You do not want to plant something only to find it has outgrown its position in a few years and is overwhelming the garden.
- Do the selected plants suit the gardens soil type? Consider the pH , drainage qualities and nutrient content of your garden soil
- Are the light levels in your garden suitable?

Planting combinations: dappled shade In an area of dappled shade, you may wish to plant a witch hazel such as wonderful *Hamamelis* x *intermedia* 'Pallida' (witch hazel). This develops into a large urn-shaped shrub with spidery yellow flowers in early spring and flame-coloured leaves in autumn. This plant could be backed by *Leycesteria formosa*, a shrub with fresh green foliage in spring, purple flowers in summer and attractive, jade-green winter stems. For underplanting the witch hazel, *Hakonechloa macra* 'Aureola', a low, spreading, golden variegated grass, and *Viburnum davidii*, a low-growing evergreen with pleated leaves, white summer flowers and

blue berries in winter, would be suitable. *Helleborus argutifolius*, with evergreen grey-green foliage and yellow-green flowers in late winter, would also fit well here. The framework is now established. Add to this blend *Polystichum setiferum*, a fern with fresh green fronds that echo the vase-like shape of the witch hazel, yellow flowered *Digitalis lutea*, with spires of blooms in summer, *Lilium henryi*, a bulb with exotic orange blooms, also in summer, and seasonal colour is provided. A *Clematis* 'Henryi' could be included to scramble up the witch hazel, adding white summer flowers. All these plants could in turn be underplanted with *Cyclamen hederifolium* for pink flowers in autumn, and snowdrops for more early spring interest, planted through a carpet of black-leaved *Ophiopogon planisicapus* 'Nigrescens', which shows off the white snowdrop flowers to their best.

Planting combinations: deep shade This is but an example of how to think when planning an area. Where shade is heavier, fewer plants will be possible. You may have a narrow border backed by a conifer hedge. Here clumps of evergreen *Euphorbia amygdaloides* var. *robbiae*, with its lime-green flowers could be mixed with yellow daffodils and the contrasting blue flowers of *Vinca minor* and white Symphytum for a spring display. Later, pink *Geranium endressii* would continue the display. Add clumps of statuesque evergreen *Iris foetidissima*, with pods of orange seeds in winter, grassy *Carex pendula*, with its elegant arching habit, and spring-flowering shrub *Mahonia aquifolium*, with yellow blooms to give year-round presence.

Dappled shade allows varied plantings featuring many different species

In deeper shade, *Geranium endressii* would brighten a dark corner

Choosing & Buying Plants

When you are picking out specimens at the garden centre or nursery, you should ensure that plants are healthy and represent good value for money. Here are a few tips and points to consider:

Choose plants that are free from weeds A few surface weeds are of no importance, but established ones show a lack of care and possibly indicate that a plant is old and thus will be harder to establish.

Avoid pot-bound plants When a plant outgrows a container it is likely to become pot-bound, where the roots encircle the inside of the pot. With trees and shrubs this may prevent the plant ever establishing properly. Mildly rootbound plants may be worth the risk as long as roots are pulled apart on planting. The best way to tell if a plant is pot-bound is to gently remove the pot.

Check for pests and disease Do not buy a plant which has obvious signs of pests (for example, aphids, whitefly) or disease (mould, mildew). It will be weaker and may spread the problem to other plants.

Never buy plants that have dried out This may seem obvious, but sometimes a plant will appear to have been

Choose garden centre plants with care, taking time to find the best ones

Poor and healthy specimens of the same nursery plant

> **TIP** Avoid buying plants which have nearly attained their full size, as they are less likely to thrive than those bought at a third to a half their full size. Equally, if the plant is too small, it will be vulnerable to damage and generally slow to grow.

watered (that is, the surface is moist) but the roots remain dry. If a plant feels light or is wilting, avoid it.

Avoid plants too small for their pots This is a problem in spring. Sometimes plants are put out on sale before they have made sufficient growth to fill a pot. They are prone to waterlogging and rotting-off at this time and may fail to establish in the garden.

Large specimen or small? Although you will want to make an initial impact in the garden, a little patience is usually repaid, especially in shade. A large specimen plant may fill a hole quickly, but it is expensive, requires much after-care and may never establish as well as a younger plant. Smaller examples will adapt to the change in conditions (from nursery to garden) quicker and get away sooner. Remember that in shade soil is dry and rooty and the key to plants surviving lies in their ability to get roots down and find sources of water and nutrient. A large plant will take a while to establish, whereas a youngster will quickly send out questing roots.

How many examples of each plant should I buy? For small area it is usual to buy only one of each plant, but where a grouped or mass effect is required, it is often best to buy in threes or fives.

Planting

Before you plant, it is vital that you prepare the area properly. Existing beds will need to be revitalised, and new beds need shaping and starting from scratch.

Establishing the border shape When planning a new border, the simplest way to decide on its shape is to use rope or even the garden hose to give some idea of how it will appear. A good alternative is to fill an old lemonade bottle with silver sand, cut a small hole in the lid and 'draw' with it on the ground.

Removing branches and erecting trellis This is the best stage to cut out any low branches to raise light levels. When attaching trellis to existing walls and fences, the most important consideration is to ensure that it is attached on battens so that it stands proud from the surface. This will then allow climbing stems to pass behind. Climbers will weigh heavy and offer significant resistance to the wind, so ensure that trellis is fixed securely. Another problem may be the upkeep of the wall or fence behind. A good tip here is to mount the trellis on hinges to allow access.

Removing the turf Once you are satisfied with the outline of a new border, the next step is to remove the turf, or whatever is currently in situ. It is best to cut up turf into small sections with a half-moon edger and lift in a piecemeal fashion with a spade. Try to retain as much topsoil as possible, as this is the most nutrient-rich layer.

Attach trellis with sufficient space for plant tendrils to climb behind the wooden battens

Cut turf with a half-moon and then lift with a spade

Initial digging The next job is to dig the entire area over thoroughly. This will be tough, especially in shade where the ground will be dry, hard and full of roots. This job should be started with a spade, and a fork used to break the clods. Small roots can be removed but thicker ones should be worked around with the aim of establishing planting pockets in between. Pick out any large stones and weeds, or debris such as leaves and rubbish.

Adding organic matter In dry shade the most essential step is to incorporate organic matter. Well-rotted horse or farmyard manure is ideal, and it is surprising how much is required. In general, a layer 8cm (3in) thick or more in bad conditions should be dug in to one spade's depth. Do not put all the manure on at this stage. An optional additive is some inorganic fertilizer

granules to promote good growth. Once the soil has been worked to a fairly even tilth, the remainder of the manure can be spread over the soil surface. This will be incorporated at planting time. The soil should be mounded into the centre of the bed, and hopefully the soil level will now have been raised, giving plants a deeper root run. If the soil is dry, this is the ideal time to give the ground a good soaking.

Weed-suppressing membrane The ground is now ready for planting. If you want to lay a weed-suppressing membrane, now is the time to do it. Apply the fabric to the soil surface and cut holes through for planting. This material allows water to pass, but will prevent most weeds. Cover it with bark chips or gravel. This will prevent you from digging the ground in future, which may be a blessing or a curse.

Weed-suppressing membranes are ideal where the ground is unlikely to receive much maintenance and where ground cover plants are to be used, but you cannot dig the ground over and the bark chips or gravel will need topping up occasionally. Certain plants such as bulbs and others that spread from the root will not be suitable, as well as those which spread by self-seeding.

Planting step-by-step

It is important to begin by ensuring that the plant is well-watered in its container. It will not establish well in your new border if it has already dried out in its pot. If necessary, plunge the plant in a bucket of water and leave it to soak for a while, ensuring that the roots do not become waterlogged.

Next, decide where you want to position the plant and dig a hole. Make sure that the hole you dig is sufficiently large for the plant you wish to accommodate. The ideal hole should be half as wide as the pot again and fractionally deeper.

Place the plant with its container into the hole to ensure that it is the correct size. If necessary, dig out a little more soil or put some back to rest the plant at the correct depth.

Loosen soil at the bottom of the hole and add a thin layer of organic matter, to give the plant plenty of nutrition and a good start as it establishes itself in its new conditions [A].

Take the plant in one hand and gently squeeze the pot from off the rootball. If slightly pot-bound, the pot may have to be cut off [B].

Carefully tease out the roots a little, especially if the plant is pot bound.

Position the plant in the hole and back-fill around it with excavated soil mixed with organic matter to improve its quality.

Firm the soil around the plant with your hands [C] or the heel of your foot – depending on the size of the area to be firmed – and water in copiously [D].

Aftercare
Mulches and mulching

In shade, mulches are of great importance, especially in dry, rooty situations. A mulch is a layer of material applied around plants, on top of the soil surface. It may be organic or inorganic and you will find they provide many benefits. Many different materials are suitable and each one has different qualities. Some of the more popular include:

Gravel and stone chippings Chipped stone and gravel are popular mulches, as they are long-lasting and there is a huge range of colours and grades available. They are not best suited to shade, as they require maintenance in autumn to remove fallen leaves. They are moisture-retentive and ideal spread over weed-suppressing membrane. However gravel also acts as an ideal seed-bed for the germination of weed seedlings, which may need picking out regularly.

Gravel is attractive as mulch in pots, and plants enjoy growing through it.

Chipped slate is a popular modern material ideal for oriental inspired themes.

Gravel, pebbles and shells – a versatile mulch

Bark chips Perhaps the most popular mulch, this is cheap, light, biodegradable and has good moisture retaining and weed suppressing qualities. However, it needs regularly topping up and can make an area appear rather sterile. It also removes nitrogen from the soil as it rots which is a drawback as nitrogen is required for good plant growth.

Crushed glass Beloved of modernist garden designers, crushed glass is a new material available in a range of colours. Despite the fact it is glass, it is safe as the

Crushed glass has decorative properties

process of manufacture rounds off sharp edges. It has similar qualities to gravel, but is expensive and may not blend well with planting in your garden.

Rotted farmyard manure This is the ideal material if you want to feed the soil and increase its moisture holding capacity. Although cheap, it is heavy and does not prevent weed growth, but it results in luxuriant plant growth. This material is ideal for use in shade.

Leafmould The 'Rolls Royce' of mulches, this is made from leaves collected together and rotted down over several years. It is ideal for shade as it is nutrient-rich, adds fibre and drainage to the soil, retains moisture, and plants love it! However, it is not easy to make, and even harder to get hold of.

Homemade compost Everyone should make compost from trimmings, mown grass and other garden waste. It is free, on-site and full of nutrients. It also holds water in the soil and thick layers (as with other organic mulches) may provide protection for tender plants in cold weather. On the downside, you may find it spreads weed seed around the garden.

When you are spreading mulch, apply it fairly thickly, up to 10cm (4in) to get the desirable benefits of water retention, frost protection and improved soil fertility. Try to avoid mulching over the crowns of plants or allowing the mulch to make contact with stems, as this will encourage rot. Never spread pure peat on the garden; this is wasteful and serves little purpose.

Watering

After you have finished planting, watering will be essential until plants become established, which may take a couple of years. Even then you must be prepared to water in particularly dry or hot periods. This is best done early or late in the day, when less moisture is lost to evaporation. A good soak every few days is better for plants and less wasteful of water than a splash around each evening.

Watering cans If you have a small garden, you may decide that a can is sufficient. This can be used with a water butt, which negates the need to draw water from the mains in all but the driest periods. Watering cans can deliver water directly where it is needed, and as such are economical.

Hoses In larger situations a hose will make work simpler, but it is important to know how to use one properly. Simply spraying water at the plant is no good at all; the water is required at the root, so it is at the soil surface that the hose should be aimed. Allow the water to puddle and ensure that the jet is not too forceful so as to dislodge or damage the plant.

Automated watering systems These are handy if you are often away from home. They are expensive but effective, delivering water directly and economically where required via small pipes.

Feeding

Plants grown directly in the ground will require less feeding than those in pots. However soil in dry shade is often particularly hungry. The best course of action is to provide annual mulches of manure in early spring around the plants. This mulch will feed, and retain water. Between mulches, the best solution is to use pelleted chicken manure, which is strong, effective and easy to apply, if a little smelly!

Also in spring, inorganic fertilizers such as Vitex and Growmore can be spread according to manufacturer's recommendations and lightly forked in.

Pelleted chicken manure is a good plant feed

Pruning techniques

Each plant will have specific pruning requirements, but certain generalisations can be made. Shrubs that are grown for their flowers will do so either on old growth made last year or on new growth made during the current season. Those that flower on old wood should not be pruned until after flowering, as the aim is to encourage maximum growth during the season for flowers next year. Those that bloom on current growth usually (but not always) do so later in the year, so prune before these flower to maximize growth this year.

Regularly deadhead spent flowers

Sometimes plants require keeping within bounds as they outgrow their allotted space. You should try to remove whole branches rather than trimming the whole plant as this way the general form, shape and natural appearance of the plant is retained.

TRAINING AND SUPPORT

Trees and shrubs Most trees and shrubs will need little attention to begin with, apart from deadheading and some limited shaping. As the plants mature they may require some pruning to keep in bounds. Some shrubs may also require additional support using stakes or stout canes as they grow.

Climbers need to be trained to trellis work, or tied to supports with twine or wire.

Herbaceous plants Many herbaceous plants that re-grow annually will require some form of support to prevent them flopping over other plants. Tie them to bamboo canes or use purpose-made wire meshes on legs which can be placed over the crown of the plant before it begins to grow away in spring.

The stems will also need cutting down with sharp secateurs in winter or in early spring if preferred, as some plants may provide attractive seedheads. Try to remove stems as close to the crown of the plant as possible.

Plants for Shade

It is often assumed that there are a limited number of plants that will grow well in shade, but in fact the range is wide and varied, especially for those who can provide good fertile soil and plenty of moisture.

In shade, foliage is perhaps more important, and certainly longer lasting, than flowers. Plants that thrive in shade often have good foliage, be it large and bold such as that of Acanthus or fine and delicate such as the foliage of many ferns. Leaves may be glossy or matt, coloured, variegated or green. It is often worth considering plants for the value of their leaves alone and viewing flowers as an added bonus. Evergreen foliage is also important and there are many evergreen plants that will thrive in shade.

There are, however, many plants that bloom in shade, and those which do are often astonishingly beautiful. If you can provide the correct conditions, Trillium, Uvularia, anemones and even the giant Himalayan lily (*Cardiocrinum giganteum*) will flourish. The cool, moist shade these plants like is perhaps one of the most desirable of all garden situations and the treasures which can flourish here are among the choicest of all garden plants.

Even in troublesome dry shade you will find plants that will provide much interest, especially if the soil can be improved. Geraniums, euphorbias, comfrey (Symphytum), holly (Ilex), ivy (Hedera) and some ferns can all succeed. Many of these plants will grow well in containers, allowing their cultivation in areas with no open ground.

The number of plants keeps growing, with breeders around the world developing new selections, along with new species introduced from the wild. Many of the plants listed here have too numerous selections and cultivars to mention; most of those listed have proved themselves to be among the most reliable, as well as the most desirable. Shade is an increasingly common garden situation and the thirst for suitable plants is as yet unquenchable.

Acanthus
Bear's breeches

Acanthus are handsome herbaceous plants both in leaf and flower, and have been admired since classical times for their architectural qualities. Those most commonly grown are easily pleased in sun or shade and are not particular about soil type, as long as it is well drained.

Once established they make large specimens, spreading through mildly invasive roots. They are ideal planted in late spring towards the front of the border to show off the handsome foliage or in front of large shrubs. They combine well with other exotic looking plants such as ferns and fatsias.

The most often planted species is *A. mollis*, a plant with large, lush green deeply cut leaves that are soft and slightly downy beneath. In summer, towering spikes of prickly purple flowers are produced, most freely in areas with some sun. The plant is well worth growing for its leaves alone which are often retained by the plant throughout mild winters; in colder areas the frost will blacken and defoliate the plant, but clumps quickly recover in spring at which

Acanthus spinosus

soil	Well drained, fertile soil. Adding well-rotted manure will result in lush foliage
watering	Needs water until established. Luxuriant foliage is in moist locations
pruning/ thinning	Little needed. Give plants a tidy in spring; faded flower spikes can look attractive until winter
general care	Appreciate a mulch of well-rotted manure in winter, especially in colder areas to protect from hard frost
pests & diseases	Slugs and snails often damage emerging leaves. Powdery mildew may attack if plant is stressed

time old, blackened leaves can be removed. *A. mollis* var. *latifolius* is larger with even more impressive glossy arching leaves. There is also a gold-leaved cultivar, *A. mollis* 'Hollards Gold' which is effective in spring when the new leaves first emerge, coloured bright yellow. This likes more care and is slower to establish. *A. spinosus* has arguably more attractive leaves; these are large but delicate looking, being finely cut and rather spiky. It flowers more freely, but does need a slightly brighter position.

Plants are easily propagated through division of crowns in spring. These should be replanted promptly, as Acanthus dislike excessive root disturbance, indeed you may find plants sulk for a while. Alternatively grow from seed.

	SPRING	SUMMER	AUTUMN	WINTER	height (cm)	spread (cm)	flower/leaf colour	
Acanthus mollis	🌿🌿🌿	🌿🌿 ●	● ● 🌿	🌿🌿🌿	150	100	▪▪	The best for heavy shade
A. mollis 'Hollards Gold'	🌿🌿🌿	🌿🌿 ●	● ● 🌿	🌿🌿🌿	150	80	▪▪	Golden foliage
A. mollis var. latifolius	🌿🌿🌿	🌿🌿🌿	● ● 🌿	🌿🌿🌿	150	150	▪▪	The largest leaves, glossy and arching
A. spinosus	🌿🌿🌿	🌿 ● ●	● ● ●	🌿🌿🌿	150	100	▪▪	Dissected foliage and floriferous

🌿 in leaf   ● flowering

Acer
Japanese maple

Many species of Acer will grow to become large trees, but some, especially those grouped loosely as 'Japanese Acers' make valuable foliage interest shrubs and small trees. All are deciduous and many display spectacular autumn colours, as well as having attractively tinted summer foliage. However it is in spring as delicate new leaves emerge that these plants are at their most attractive.

Acers grow best in sheltered sites away from the wind, and like a moist, fertile, well-drained position. They prefer neutral to acid conditions, but some will grow on in alkaline soil as long as it is deep and moist. Many thrive in containers, indeed this is a good way to grow these plants, buying smaller, cheaper examples and letting them grow on before planting out. There is a vast range of cultivars available, most of which are derived from *A. japonicum* or *A. palmatum*, and it is really a matter of personal taste which ones are most appealing. Some form small, open, trees, others may grow into dome-shaped shrubs in time. As they do have differing characteristics and growth habits, it is worth identifying the ones which appeal to you most.

Acers associate well with a wide range of other plants. Try underplanting darker

Acer palmatum f. *atropurpureum*

Acer japonica 'Aconitifolium'

soil	Moist, rich, well drained soil, ideally neutral to acid. Tolerate good alkaline soils
watering	Never let plants dry out, or foliage suffers and plants may even die
pruning/ thinning	No pruning or thinning is generally required, apart from the exception to re-shape or cut it to size
general care	Cover plants with fleece if frosts threaten emerging foliage. Ensure potted specimens do not dry out
pests & diseases	Aphids sometimes attack young growth, and watch for scale insect. There are no other problems

leaved cultivars with gold-leaved plants such as the wonderful grass Hakonechola or dwarf holly *Ilex crenata* 'Golden Gem'. These plants are easy to grow from seed. Grafting is an alternative but trickier method.

Acer palmatum var. *dissectum*

	SPRING	SUMMER	AUTUMN	WINTER	height (cm)	spread (cm)	leaf colour	
Acer japonicum 'Aconitifolium'	🍂🍂	🍂🍂	🍂🍂		500	600		Larger cultivar with distinctive foliage; turns red in autumn
A. palmatum f. atropurpureum	🍂🍂	🍂🍂	🍂🍂		800	600		Deeply lobed red leaves
A. palmatum 'Bloodgood'	🍂🍂	🍂🍂	🍂		500	500		Good richly coloured foliage
A. palmatum var. dissectum	🍂🍂	🍂🍂	🍂🍂		200	300		Mound forming selection. Gold leaves in autumn
A. palmatum 'Osakasuki'	🍂🍂	🍂🍂	🍂🍂		600	600		Has large deeply lobed foliage; good autumn tints
A. shirasawanum 'Aureum'	🍂🍂	🍂🍂	🍂		400	400		Slow but beautiful, with little golden, fan-like leaves

🍂 *in leaf*

Aconitum

Monkshood *or*
Wolf's bane

With sinister-looking spikes of hooded, usually blue or white flowers, these relatives of the delphinium are a great asset in shade, although it is important to treat them with caution, for all parts of these plants are poisonous.

Most produce tuberous roots and begin growth early in the season; the fresh divided green leaves are a useful foil around early flowering plants such as snowdrops. The dark-flowered kinds look good against light backdrops such as white painted walls, where the rather sinister charms of their hooded flowers may be more easily seen.

Aconitums will grow in most soils, although best results will be had in rich, moist ground. Taller selections will need staking when grown in shade, this is best carried out while clumps are developing, early in the season. Cut down faded stems to the ground once the leaves have started to turn yellow, usually in mid autumn.

A. carmichaelii 'Arendsii' will reach 1.2m (4ft), with rich blue flowers carried on short spikes. These are produced in autumn, when blue flowers are in short supply.

Among the most dramatic of monkshoods is *A. camarum* 'Bicolor' with flowers of purplish-blue and white in mid-late summer. Some aconitums such as *A. hemsleyanum* are herbaceous climbers and will scramble happily through shrubs, producing unusual blue flowers, perhaps contrasting with the supporting plant. Try it with a golden-leaved elder, or use it to spice up a plant that has gone out of season. Propagation is through division of clumps in late autumn.

Aconitum napellus

Aconitum 'Spark's Variety'

soil	Most soils, acid or alkaline; plants grow best in moist, rich conditions
watering	Water until established. Tolerate some drought, but performance is hindered
pruning/ thinning	Cut stems after foliage has turned yellow. Divide in late autumn every 3–4 years for taller flower stems
general care	Plants like a mulch of organic matter in spring, and taller selections may require some staking
pests & diseases	Relatively trouble free. There are not usually any problems regarding pests and diseases

	SPRING	SUMMER	AUTUMN	WINTER	height (cm)	spread (cm)	flower colour	
A. x camarum 'Bicolor'	in leaf	in leaf / flowering	in leaf	in leaf	120	50		Striking blooms and good habit
Aconitum carmichaelii 'Arendsii'	in leaf	in leaf	flowering / in leaf	in leaf	120	30		Wonderful flowers contrast against autumn tints
A. hemsleyanum	in leaf	in leaf / flowering	in leaf	in leaf	150	50		Climbing species. Grown through shrubs for support
A. napellus	in leaf	in leaf / flowering	in leaf	in leaf	150	30		Probably the best species for dryer, darker conditions
A. 'Sparks Variety'	in leaf	flowering	flowering / in leaf	in leaf	150	50		A fine, long-flowering cultivar with sultry flowers

in leaf   flowering

Adiantum
Maidenhair fern

These are beautiful ferns; the individual leaflets are so thin, they tremble in the slightest breeze. However, most are rather tougher than their almost impossibly delicate appearance would suggest, although they must have constantly moist but not waterlogged soil and need protection from drying winds. Indeed, these plants are most happy where the humidity is constantly high, such as by a stream.

Adiantums do best in a cool climate and will tolerate alkaline soil as long as it is rich in organic matter. In mild conditions the two species mentioned here tend to retain some foliage over winter, but it becomes rather tatty, and in colder areas both will die back to the crown, only to re-sprout in spring. They grow well in combination with other ferns or slow-growing plants that will emphasize their delicate appearance, such as Ajuga, Cyclamen or Ophiopogon. Large specimens may be split in late summer or early spring to increase them, but ensure resulting divisions are not too small, and do not plant deeply as this will cause crowns to rot and plants to die. Bear this in mind also if mulching around established plants; remember to leave a gap around the plant. An easy way to do this is to cover the plant

with an upturned flowerpot until you have finished spreading whatever you are mulching with.

Adiantum capillis-veneris is the larger and more tender species. Although it is actually a British native plant, it should be grown only in sheltered areas. Tougher and more adaptable *A. aleuticum*, often wrongly sold as *A. pedatum* (a much rarer species), is far hardier and has attractive, divided fronds.

Adiantum capillis-veneris

soil	Moist, humus rich but well drained soil; dislikes growing on in chalky areas
watering	Never allow the plant to dry out, and grow in a humid atmosphere
pruning/ thinning	Remove old tatty fronds to crown in early spring; however, little else is ever required
general care	Generally easy to maintain. Plants like an annual mulch, but do not apply material over the crowns
pests & diseases	Slugs and snails may munch on emerging fronds in spring, but there are no other problems

Adiantum aleuticum

	SPRING	SUMMER	AUTUMN	WINTER	height (cm)	spread (cm)	leaf colour	
Adiantum aleuticum					60	50		Probably the best species for garden cultivation
A. capillis-veneris					40	50		Rather tender, but good for sheltered places

⊘ in leaf

Ajuga
Bugle

These low-growing plants make excellent small-scale ground cover in shady areas with their dark, textured leaves and spires of purple flowers in early summer. They spread by runners that form new plantlets when they touch the ground.

soil	Grows best in rich conditions. When happy, plants multiply and spread
watering	Keep plants from drying out, giving extra water in summer if required
pruning/ thinning	No pruning is usually required; if the plant spreads too far, simply remove plantlets
general care	Almost maintenance free; plants are improved if dead leaves are removed and an annual mulch applied
pests & diseases	Slugs and snails may attack plants, and watch for powdery mildew in summer. There are no other problems

These plants can be a little particular; however, give them a moist spot with good, well-drained soil and they will spread happily. For the lushest growth, mulch plants well with rotted farmyard manure in spring, tickling it through the mats of plants. Use these plants underneath other taller plants, or grow bulbs such as Narcissus through them. They are ideal at the front of borders, forming a natural-looking, even neat edging. Simply trim off any plantlets which grow out of place.

Some selections of Ajuga have darker leaves, a colour that is even more intense if plants receive a little sun. Ajugas are not terribly vigorous if in less than ideal conditions; do be sure plants do not get overrun by other strong-growing bed-fellows.

Ajuga 'Catlins Giant'

Ajuga 'Catlins Giant' is one of the largest cultivars, and is most attractive in flower, the flowers appearing in late spring. It has large greenish-bronze leaves. *A. reptans* is rather smaller and quite variable, some selections having particularly dark purple leaves.

Ajugas are suited to growing in mixed planters acting as a foil for other larger plants, and spilling over the edges of containers. They work particularly well with evergreen plants, the dark leaved selections providing a good contrast with golden variegated Euonymus or with *Luzula* 'Hohe Tatra'.

Propagation is easy: simply detach plantlets once they start to root and re-plant.

Ajuga reptans

	SPRING	SUMMER	AUTUMN	WINTER	height (cm)	spread (cm)	flower/leaf colour	
Ajuga 'Catlins Giant'					20	100		Most substantial selection
A. reptans					15	100		Remove old flower spikes with shears in summer.

in leaf   flowering

Amelanchier

This genus of large deciduous shrubs and small trees contains some excellent plants for the small, modern garden where plants have to earn their keep. Many have attractive, white, star-shaped flowers in spring which are followed by reddish fruits that appear in autumn.

However, these plants' finest quality is that the small, oval leaves turn brilliant colours before falling, creating a spectacular display. Amelanchiers are hardy, easy to grow and as trees will not get too large for most gardens, although they do best in moist but well drained acidic soils. Some also relish shade, although they will not thrive in the darkest positions. The bright colours of the autumn leaves provide interest among evergreen rhododendrons, Pieris and camellias. Amelanchiers are perhaps least interesting during the summer, and so should be grown with plants that will provide attractive flowers and leaves at this time. Plants are quite quick-growing and eventually will produce suckers and form a thicket. The suckers can be detached with some root, and used to increase the plant. Alternatively layer the branches or grow plants from seed sown in late autumn or early spring.

Amelanchier canadensis is a large, shrubby species which grows best in a moist

Amelanchier canadensis

soil	Grow best in acid soil that is well drained, but will take less-than perfect positions
watering	Keep plants well-watered when establishing. Tolerates dryness after a few years
pruning/ thinning	Remove badly positioned or crossing branches in early spring, before plants come into growth
general care	A general spring shaping is helpful, and plants enjoy a mulch of organic matter, especially on drier soils
pests & diseases	Watch for dying leaves and flowers, and oozing of liquid from stems. This could be fireblight; there is no cure

soil, with pure white flowers and leaves that turn orange in autumn. *A. lamarkii* is perhaps the most often offered: it is a small tree, with white flowers and attractive bronze coloured young leaves in spring. Leaves turn a rich red before falling. It will tolerate drier conditions than *A.canadensis*.

Amelanchier lamarkii

	SPRING	SUMMER	AUTUMN	WINTER	height (cm)	spread (cm)	flower/leaf colour	
Amelanchier canadensis	✳ 🍃	🍃 🍃 🍃	🍃 🍃		600	300	▯	Produces suckers; remove to retain a tree-like appearance
A. lamarkii	✳ 🍃	🍃 🍃 🍃	🍃 🍃		1000	1200	▮	Larger and more tree like in its growth habit

🍃 in leaf   ✳ flowering

Anemone
Windflower

This large genus of herbaceous plants contains many popular in the garden. Most come from woodlands, and thus are ideally suited to the shaded garden. Of those commonly grown, it is the larger, late-flowering ones which create the greatest impact, but there are many smaller and charming spring flowering species to consider as well.

Anemone blanda

The spring flowering anemones such as *Anemone blanda* and *A. nemerosa* are low-growing plants which spread by fleshy rhizomatous roots. *A. nemerosa* is the first to flower, the blooms opening in early spring. They are usually white but maybe pink or blue, and double forms are often sold. Plants are easy to grow in almost any soil, even heavy clay, so long as it is not waterlogged, and they do well under other plants. By summer the leaves die away completely. *A. blanda* is smaller and flowers later; again in white, mauve-blue or pinkish-red, it likes similar conditions.

Autumn flowering anemones are larger plants with attractive luxuriant foliage and a long flowering period. The pinkish or white blooms are held on tall stems that seldom

soil	Moist, well drained soil with added organic matter, Survives in poorer soils
watering	Established plants survive some drought. Luxuriate with moisture at root
pruning/ thinning	Larger autumn flowering kinds need cutting to the ground in winter; clumps can be divided in spring
general care	Provide an annual mulch for the best plants; the taller Japanese anemones may need staking
pests & diseases	Slugs and snails, also leaf eelworms in Japanese anemones. In dryer conditions, powdery mildew

Anemone nemerosa

require staking and can often be seen up until the first frosts, making them valuable in the garden.

In shade perhaps the finest of all is *A. x hybrida* 'Honorine Joubert', a wonderful, strong growing plant with stout stems holding masses of pure white flowers which have an illuminating presence. They grow in acid or alkaline soil and spread slowly but strongly from the root, forming large clumps. They will survive in quite poor conditions – some even in dry shade once established – but they are far better with some moisture and a regular application of well-rotted manure. Propagate them from division in spring.

	SPRING	SUMMER	AUTUMN	WINTER	height (cm)	spread (cm)	flower colour	
Anemone blanda	flowering/in leaf	in leaf	in leaf		10	20		Charming spring flower; the leaves die down in summer
A. hupehensis 'Hadspen Abundance'		in leaf	in leaf/flowering	flowering	70	50		Similar to *x. hybrida* cultivars; more intense flower colour
A. x hybrida 'Honorine Joubert'		in leaf	in leaf/flowering	flowering	150	80		The best white cultivar; in bloom for over 3 months
A. x hybrida 'Queen Charlotte'		in leaf	in leaf/flowering	flowering	150	80		Vigorous selection with long flowering season
A. x hybrida 'September Charm'		in leaf	in leaf/flowering	flowering	80	80		Good strong flower colour. Short flower stems
A. x hybrida 'Whirlwind'		in leaf	in leaf/flowering	flowering	100	80		Double flowers, usually shorter
A. nemerosa	flowering	in leaf			12	30		Leaves die down in mid-summer

in leaf   *flowering*

Angelica archangelica

These members of the cow-parsley family are becoming increasingly popular in gardens, thanks to their ease of cultivation and dramatic architectural qualities. Many like a sunny position, but *Angelica archangelica* will grow well in shade.

It is a biennial species (dies down after flowering in the second year) but is very easy to grow from seed, and quickly makes an attractive plant, with clumps of large, pale green leaves. In the second year a huge flowering stem reaching 1.8m (6ft) develops in early summer, bearing clusters of rounded football-sized flowerheads of small green flowers. These are followed by thousands of seeds, which spread around the garden. The best policy here is to collect some before they fall and sow them straight away in pots of compost. Resulting plants can be positioned where required later in the season, and unwanted self-sown seedlings removed. The stem can be retained before the seeds finish falling, as it remains attractive.

Once a plant the size of this species is removed from the border, it can leave quite a gap, so make sure you have something substantial to replace it with waiting in the wings. As a result, placing this plant in the garden can be a little tricky; try allowing it at the front of a border where it can be well appreciated until it goes over.

soil	Rich, moist and well drained will give the biggest plants, but not fussy over pH
watering	Keep plants well watered at all times, but do not waterlog them
pruning/ thinning	None really needed, except once plant has flowered and died, when it should be removed
general care	Plant in late summer and mulch in spring. Stop small plants flowering by removing flowering stems
pests & diseases	Slugs and snails are a real menace, as is blackfly, especially in spring. There are no other problems

These plants like a moist, rich soil, acid or alkaline. It is the candied stems of this plant which are used as cake decoration. Slugs and snails also find this plant most attractive, eating holes in leaves and stems, so be on the look out for these pests.

Angelica archangelica

Arisaema

These strange but intriguing plants are well worth the extra attention they deserve, and will grow well in shade. An increasing range of species is becoming available as they become more popular, but do ensure that plants you buy have not been taken from the wild.

Arisaemas are members of the arum-lily family and originate in North America and Japan, growing in moist woodland, conditions that must be replicated in the garden if they are to flourish. They grow from tubers that are best planted in pots in spring and started off in a cold frame or a sheltered corner with some protection outside. Plant out into a sheltered spot with a well drained, rich soil, improving if possible with leaf mould. Perhaps most attractive and widely available is beautiful *Arisaema candidissimum*, with spathes of white and pale pink followed by large tri-lobed leaves.

Growth above ground does not start until summer with this species, so don't panic if it does not appear with other spring flowers. Green *A. triphyllum* is a good one to start

Arisaema triphyllum

Arisaema candidissimum

soil	Plants need well-drained gritty soil with added leaf mould. They like a cool spot
watering	Make sure plants are moist in summer. Keep them on dry side in winter if possible
pruning/ thinning	There are no specific pruning or thinning regimes for this plant, as it does not need any
general care	Add leaf mould mulch in spring. Plants are best bought in growth rather than as dry tubers
pests & diseases	Slugs and snails. Plants in wet positions will rot over winter. Plants in pots may be attacked by vine weevil

with, being easy to grow. Next, you could try purplish *A. consanguneum*, that also has wonderful leaves resembling a parasol, or bizarre-looking and rather tender *A. nepenthoides*, with brown, spotted flowers early in the season.

Plants are propagated from young tubers that are produced during the season. These are best removed and potted up in gritty compost and grown on until large enough to flower, which may take a couple of years. Sometimes, flowers are followed by spikes of usually red berries, that may be sown when ripe in autumn.

	SPRING	SUMMER	AUTUMN	WINTER	height (cm)	spread (cm)	flower/leaf colour	
Arisaema candidissimum		❀ 🍃 🍃 🍃			50	50	▮	The most attractive. Plant deep and wait until early summer
A. consanguineum		❀ 🍃 🍃 🍃 🍃			80	40	▮	Mottled foliage of this plant is attractive. Likes warm spot
A. nepenthoides	❀	🍃 🍃 🍃 🍃 🍃			60	40	▮	Plant must have warm, sheltered position. It flowers early
A. triphyllum		❀ 🍃 🍃 🍃 🍃			30	30	▮	The easiest to grow in normal garden conditions

 🍃 in leaf   ❀ flowering

Arum

Similar to Arisaema, but more often seen and rather less choosy over growing conditions, the arum most often seen in cultivation, *A. italicum* subsp. *italicum* 'Marmoratum', is an essential plant for winter interest in the shaded garden, providing much-needed fresh and bright foliage at a most unseasonable time.

These easy, low-growing herbaceous plants with tuberous roots begin growth in mid-winter, sending up fresh-looking, rather lush, sparkling arrowhead-shaped green leaves centred with silver. These plants are remarkably tough, often being frosted to the ground, but soon recovering in a thaw. They make a pleasing clump in almost any soil, even taking some drought, especially in summer when they naturally die down. Team

soil	Not fussy. Will grow well in a wide range of soils, so long as not waterlogged
watering	Should be moist in growing season. Tolerates drought in summer as foliage withers
pruning/ thinning	Remove dead vegetation during late summer dormancy. Little other care is needed
general care	Spring mulches show off the foliage. Do retain flowers, as they often lead to autumn displays of berries
pests & diseases	Relatively trouble free. There are not usually any problems regarding pests and diseases

Arum italicum 'Marmoratum'

Arum italicum 'Chameleon'

up the silvery foliage with the flowers of a good, strong snowdrop such as *Galanthus* 'Sam Arnott' and underplant with the black-leaved *Ophiopogon planisicapus* 'Nigrescens'.

Typical green arum flowers appear in early summer, after which the foliage begins to wane and eventually dies back, when it should be removed. In autumn, spikes of red, yellow and orange berries appear, which make a wonderful show, especially teamed with purple colchicums or *Cyclamen hederifolium*. The berries easily germinate and grow into more plants. Alternatively split clumps in spring or summer. *A.* 'Chameleon' produces larger, more rounded leaves that have greyish markings on them, while *A.* 'White Winter' should be sought for its most dramatic foliage brightly centred with silver.

	SPRING	SUMMER	AUTUMN	WINTER	height (cm)	spread (cm)	leaf colour	
Arum 'Chameleon'	🌿🌿✹			🌿🌿🌿	50	50		Larger rounded leaves
A. italicum 'Marmoratum'	🌿🌿✹			🌿🌿🌿	50	50		Looks fantastic with snowdrops. An essential garden plant
A. italicum 'White Winter'	🌿🌿✹			🌿🌿🌿	40	40		A selection with the strongest variegation.

🌿 in leaf   ✹ flowering

Asplenium scolopendrium
Hart's tongue fern

This elegant plant is one of the simplest of all ferns to grow, and will thrive in a wide range of sites, although it is usually best in shade in an alkaline soil. It will tolerate poor conditions, indeed it is often seen growing from almost bare rock in the wild.

This easy plant must not get too dry, but is the fern to try if you have really deep shade. In these conditions give plants a thick annual mulch in spring to help hold moisture in. Asplenium is at its most attractive in spring when the young crosiers (unfurling fronds) emerge from the central crown. The fronds are not divided up like most other ferns, but are strap-like, gloriously shiny and verdant – a luminous apple green in colour. It is at this stage that late frost may cause damage, but usually it is very hardy, indeed it is a British native.

This fern is just about evergreen, although by late winter the plant usually looks pretty tatty and is best relieved of last season's growth, that will now be limp and lying flat. Do this when the new growth appears. Grow Asplenium with hostas and other plants that have much more rounded leaves to provide a welcome contrast in leaf shape, or mix with spring flowers such as hellebores or leucojums, where the emerging leaves will form an elegant foil. There are many named selections of this plant with leaves that are ruffled or undulated, but for my money, the unadulterated species is the finest.

soil	Best in free-draining, moist organic rich soil; prefers alkaline, but grows in acid
watering	Will take more dryness than some ferns, but plant will suffer after a while
pruning/ thinning	Remove tatty fronds as new crosiers emerge in spring. There is little else required in terms of pruning
general care	Generally easy to maintain and cultivate. Mulch in spring, but be careful of delicate new growth
pests & diseases	Relatively trouble free. There are not usually any problems regarding pests and diseases

Asplenium scolopendrium

Athyrium
Lady fern

These lovely deciduous ferns are easily grown in moist shade, although _Athyrium filix-femina_ will also adapt to fairly dry conditions. The fronds of this species are an attractive fresh green in spring, and are finely divided, creating a wonderful lacy effect.

The only downside is that by summer, especially in hot seasons, plants are prone to becoming rather bedraggled. However, do resist the temptation to remove fronds early, especially in cold regions, as it is best to retain old dead fronds over winter to protect the crown from heavy frost. Plants seed around and young plants can be moved and replanted elsewhere when found. Grow the lady fern with other stalwarts of the shade garden, especially evergreen shrubs such as Aucuba that will benefit from the fern's light, delicate touch. It is attractive, also, with _Euphorbia amygdaloides_ var. _robbiae_, the lime-green flowers blending with the fern's emerging fronds. Add in _Tellima grandiflora_ to continue the theme.

Rather different and arguably more refined is the Japanese painted fern, _Athyrium niponicum_ var. _pictum_. This slower-growing species has arching fronds

Athyrium filix-femina

Athyrium niponicum var. _pictum_

soil	Moist, acid or alkaline soil, with organic matter. _A.felix-femina_ takes poorer soils
watering	Keep plants moist. Plants can look tatty quite early if allowed to dry out
pruning/ thinning	Remove old fronds in spring, they help protect the plant overwinter. Little else is required
general care	Mulch in spring if possible, but avoid the crowns especially of _A. niponicum_ var. _pictum_
pests & diseases	Relatively trouble free. As there are not usually any problems regarding pests and diseases

of dark maroon, overlaid with silvery-grey, and is a most refined plant. It really needs moist, rich soil and a spot where it will be pampered to give of its best. As this fern dies down completely and emerges rather late in spring, it is worth marking the position of the clump so that you don't try and plant something on top of it. Mix it with choice woodland plants such as epimediums and the white-flowered form of _Cyclamen hederifolium_, or plants with golden foliage.

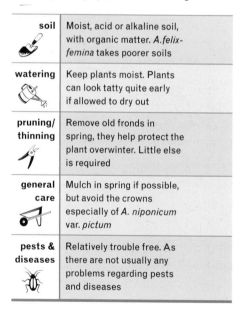

	SPRING	SUMMER	AUTUMN	WINTER	height (cm)	spread (cm)	leaf colour	
Athyrium filix-femina	🌿🌿	🌿🌿🌿	🌿		60	60		Dainty leaves are lovely fresh green in spring
Athyrium niponicum var. _pictum_	🌿🌿	🌿🌿🌿	🌿		30	30		Foliage shown off best with golden leaved plants

🌿 _in leaf_

Aucuba
Spotted laurel

These evergreen shrubs were popular with the Victorians. Justly so, for they are fine foliage plants, putting up with all manner of mistreatment, yet producing attractive, usually spotted leaves and clusters of eye-catching red berries in spring.

They will survive in terrible rooty soil in dry shade, even beneath evergreens, where the gold spotting on the leaves provides valuable colour. If they get too large they can be cut back without worry, and they also grow well in containers. The drab spikes of flowers appear in summer. For a good crop of berries you will need plants of different sexes, although these plants are seen in many gardens, so the chances of cross pollination are high. Plants may suffer in very cold winters, emerging foliage blackened by frost, but they usually recover.

Plant Aucuba towards the back of a shady border and blend in plants with golden leaves and white such as *Philadelphus coronarious* 'Aureus' or *Choisya ternata* 'Sundance' for a bright, uplifting combination. As the aucuba leaves are rather large and solid, the addition of bamboos or, at a lower level, even ferns, will help introduce a lighter feel. *Aucuba japonica* 'Crotonifolia' is most often seen; look out for *A. japonica* 'Picturata', in which leaves have a striking

Aucuba japonica 'Crotonifolia'

Aucuba japonica 'Rozzanie'

Aucuba japonica

soil	Any, even dry, poor soil and clay, regardless of pH. Best in moist, well drained loam
watering	Plants will tolerate dry shade where almost nothing else will survive
pruning/ thinning	Plants may need to be restricted in size – simply remove offending branches – but little else is required
general care	Easy to grow, may be affected by hard frost in cold regions. An annual mulch will be appreciated
pests & diseases	Relatively trouble free. There are not usually any problems with pests and diseases

gold 'flash' in their centres, or *A. japonica* 'Rozzanie' – a compact plant with rich green, glossy leaves which is valuable for the copious amounts of large red berries it produces. Propagate from semi-ripe cuttings in summer and look out for self-sow seedlings around mature plants.

	SPRING	SUMMER	AUTUMN	WINTER	height (cm)	spread (cm)	leaf colour	
Aucuba japonica 'Crotonifolia'	🌿🌿🌿	🌿🌿🌿	🌿🌿🌿	🌿🌿🌿	250	200		An all round winner in problem places. Good in a pot too
A. japonica 'Picturata'	🌿🌿🌿	🌿🌿🌿	🌿🌿🌿	🌿🌿🌿	150	200		Striking variegation illuminates dark spots
A. japonica 'Rozzanie'	🌿🌿🌿	🌿🌿🌿	🌿🌿🌿	🌿🌿🌿	100	100		Grow for glossy leaves and fine red berries in spring

🌿 *in leaf*

Begonia

Begonias are usually thought of as a tender genus of plants suitable for indoor cultivation, but surprisingly, a few are actually quite hardy. These varieties will live quite happily in a shady environment, unlike the majority of begonias.

The best for garden use is *Begonia grandis* subsp. *evansiana*. This plant begins growth in early summer from bulbils which overwinter underground. It produces exotic-looking, gleaming red-tinged leaves during the summer, and in early autumn, pendent clusters of pinkish flowers. This plant is best positioned towards the front of beds and borders, as it never reaches more than about 40cm high. The only real drawback is that this begonia only actually gets going by mid-summer, looking its best just before the frosts, so it is not best suited to regions prone to early frosts. To get the maximum growth from this species, give it a moist, rich soil with plenty of added organic matter, and plant somewhere sheltered. Keep well watered in summer and provide a thick overwintering mulch of well rotted manure to protect the bulbils from hard frost. This is no plant for dry or excessively shaded spots, but in moist, light shade it lends an air of the exotic.

The white-flowered selection has greener foliage but the same requirements, while in shade the flowers are more

soil	Soil should be rich, moist and well drained, which suits these plants best
watering	The more water applied in summer, the lusher the foliage, if not waterlogged
pruning/ thinning	No specific pruning regimes. Tidy away dead material when plants dies back at the end of summer
general care	A thick overwintering mulch of well rotted mature will protect the roots, but otherwise, little else is required
pests & diseases	Watch for slug and snail attack, but there are no other problems regarding pests and diseases

B. grandis subsp. *evansiana* var. *alba*

effective. Plant these wonderful begonias with ferns or with grassy leaved plants, where the rounded foliage shows up best. These plants are superb planted under tree ferns for a superbly tropical effect.

Propagate this plant by removing young plants growing from small bulbils in spring. It is best to pot these up in well drained compost and grow small plants on for a year or so.

Begonia grandis subsp. *evansiana*

	SPRING	SUMMER	AUTUMN	WINTER	height (cm)	spread (cm)	flower/leaf colour	
Begonia grandis subsp. *evansiana*		🌿 🌿 🌿 ✹	✹		30	40		Adds exotic touch to garden. Needs shelter
B. grandis subsp. *evansiana* var. *alba*		🌿 🌿 🌿 ✹	✹		30	40		The white blooms show up well in shade

🌿 in leaf   ✹ flowering

Berberidopsis corallina
Coral plant

This choice evergreen climbing plant can be a tricky customer, but is well worth the effort, if you can provide it with the conditions it likes. Firstly it must have an acid soil which never dries out, yet is well-drained enough to prevent waterlogging.

Added organic material, preferably leaf mould, will help it grow well. Plant it on a cool wall, shaded but sheltered from drying winds and winter frosts, and give it trellis to climb on. If you have the right conditions, this wonderful species will need little attention, needing no pruning, although shoots often need tying in. Unfortunately the plant is seldom a success in a container – the roots simply get too warm and dry in summer. If you really want to try this technique of growing, choose a large container and position in a cool shaded spot, and water regularly.

Why go to all this trouble? This plant comes from parts of Chile and is a most refined character, producing rich green, oval, lightly toothed evergreen leaves on delicate stems. In summer, small drooping clusters of rounded, rich red flowers are produced over several weeks, dangling from beneath the foliage. They are shiny and most eye-catching. This climber is at its best planted on its own, with perhaps slow-growing plants growing around the base. Try plants with reddish or purplish foliage to highlight the red flowers, and perhaps add some gold into the palette to provide a brighter tone.

Propagation is difficult and best left to the experts, although layering the stems will eventually prove successful, taking several years before rooting.

Berberidopsis corallina

soil	Fussy. Needs a well drained, moist, acidic, cool soil. Plants fail in any other soil
watering	Must never dry out. Keep the plant moist, but not waterlogged
pruning/ thinning	There are no specific pruning or thinning regimes for this plant, except for re-shaping if required
general care	This is a tricky plant and only for you if conditions are right. It is rather tender, so must have a sheltered wall
pests & diseases	Relatively trouble free. There are not usually any problems regarding pests and diseases

Berberis
Barberry

These prickly, easy-to-grow shrubs are of high value in the shaded garden, and are unfussy as to soil requirements, so long as they are not waterlogged. Some will even take poor, dry, rooty conditions, while many are successful on heavy, clay soil.

Berberis are remarkably long-suffering, withstanding cold winds, heavy frost and general neglect, although it is a shame to treat them badly, as grown well they can make a fine contribution in the garden. If grown in a reasonable soil, kept well-watered and provided with an annual mulch of well rotted manure, they often make spectacular plants.

The genus is quite varied; some are evergreen, others deciduous, the leaves of the latter usually showing fine autumn colours before falling. They also produce berries, which are attractive, but they are generally grown either for foliage such as *Berberis thunbergii* 'Golden Ring' with purple, oval leaves edged with gold, or flowers, such as the popular *B. darwinii*, with its clusters of hanging, orange blossoms. This species (and many others) is most attractive planted on a bank so that the dangling flowers and arching habit can be easily appreciated. Some berberis such as erect *B. thunbergii* 'Hellmond Pillar' have interesting form and combine well with other plants, especially those of a rounded outline,

such as clipped box globes, providing fine contrast of form. Most can be easily shaped and pruned if they get too large and they can also be useful for providing spiky boundary planting, deterring trespassers.

These plants associate well with many garden plants, the dark leaved selections

soil	Can survive dry conditions, or heavy clay. Moisture and organic matter is best
watering	Plants will withstand some drought, but do better in a moist soil
pruning/ thinning	Some Berberis can be used as a hedge or shaped into balls. Does not respond well to a hard prune
general care	Easy and trouble free. A mulch will be appreciated, especially in poor, dry conditions
pests & diseases	Mildew can affect some species, but there are not usually any problems with pests and diseases

Berberis darwinii

can be planted with gold and variegated plants for a rich spread of foliage colour. They also form a fine backdrop for planting, especially the evergreen varieties.

Berberis are good hosts for climbing plants such as Clematis. Some berberis can be clipped and shaped, adding a touch of formality into shady areas.

Propagate plants from seed in autumn.

Berberis darwinii

Berberis thunbergii atropurpurea

Deciduous types can be struck from soft wood or semi ripe cuttings in summer, the evergreen ones by semi ripe cuttings, also in summer. These should root by autumn and can be planted out into final positions the following spring.

Try scrambling white flowered *Clematis* 'Henryi' over a purple-leaved berberis, or for a more subtle combination allow a climbing Aconitum to twine through berberis for extra late summer colour.

Combine the strong forms of clipped berberis with more delicate looking ferns, golden Millium or Hakonechloa, or else team with bolder bergenias or even hellebores.

Worthy of special mention, *B. wilsoniae* has particularly fine displays of coral coloured berries that follow small yellow flowers. It is recommended for even small gardens because it is compact and is spectacular once the leaves begin to fall.

	SPRING	SUMMER	AUTUMN	WINTER	height (cm)	spread (cm)	flower/leaf colour	
Berberis darwinii	leaf/flowering	in leaf	in leaf	in leaf	300	300	▪	Evergreen species with orange flowers in spring
B. x ottawensis f. purpurea 'Superba'	in leaf	flowering/leaf	in leaf		250	200	▪	Fine red autumn colour
B. x stenophylla	in leaf flowering	in leaf	in leaf	in leaf	250	250	▪	Quick growing, evergreen plant with scented flowers
B. thunbergii atropurpurea	flowering	in leaf	in leaf		300	200	▪	Deciduous, but brightly coloured leaves. Better on acid soils
B. thunbergii 'Golden Ring'	flowering	in leaf	in leaf		200	150	▪	A charming plant, the leaves seem to sparkle
B. thunbergii 'Hellmond Pillar'	flowering	in leaf	in leaf		150	300	▪	Columnar plant, ideal for adding contrast to the garden
B. wilsoniae	flowering	in leaf	in leaf		100	150	▪	Wonderful autumnal displays of leaf colour and red berries

 in leaf   ● flowering

Bergenia
Elephant's ears

With bold, often evergreen foliage that in some cases turns attractive colours in winter, and short spikes of pretty white or pink flowers in early spring, bergenias are useful to have in the garden. They make fine ground cover, slowly spreading via rhizomes above the soil, under and around shrubs and trees.

Bergenia cordifolia

Bergenia are not particular over soil conditions, as long as it is not waterlogged. In deep shade the leaves will not assume the attractive burnished hues seen on those grown in full sun, but equally some degree of shade provides protection from frost for the flowers that are often blackened early in the season. They are wonderful when used in contrast with strappy leaves of, for instance, *Iris foetidissima*, or used as a foil for plants with delicate, divided leaves. They look good at the front of borders spilling over paths, softening hard edging, or can be used as repeat plants, providing a sense of rhythm.

Bergenia will tolerate rather dry conditions with ease and may be tried in dry shade, although they will need some extra water. For the best plants, mulch well with manure in spring and remove old blackening leaves regularly. One species is worth special mention: *Bergenia ciliata*, a magnificent plant that is rather more tender than the others, growing huge leaves which are covered with fine hairs.

Bergenia 'Morgenröte'

soil	Will grow in poor dry soil. *B. ciliata* needs a moist, rich, well-drained soil
watering	Plants are lushest if well watered. Are able to withstand drought
pruning/ thinning	Plants need rejuvenating every 3–4 years as rhizomes become long are bare. Little else is required
general care	A spring mulch maintains growth. Remove old leaves. Spring flowers are often frosted
pests & diseases	Not usually a problem, although snails hide in them. Vine weevil can sometimes attack

	SPRING	SUMMER	AUTUMN	WINTER	height (cm)	spread (cm)	flower/leaf colour	
Bergenia 'Abenglut'					25	30		Has short flower spikes. Leaves maroon in winter
B. ciliata					30	50		Handsome species worth extra effort for large hairy leaves
B. cordifolia					50	80		One of the toughest of all, if a little uninspiring
B. 'Morgenröte'					40	50		Has large flowers on tall stems, sometimes twice a year
B. purpurascens					35	30		Leaves turn purple in winter. Neat habit
B. x scmidtii					40	70		Broad leaves with long stalks, early pink flowers
B. 'Silberlicht'					40	60		Good for heads of white flowers, sometimes shy to bloom
B. 'Wintermarchen'					40	60		Rich flowers, good winter colour

🌿 *in leaf*   ☀ *flowering*

Blechnum
Hard fern

These elegant ferns are largely from a rather tender genus, but at least two species make fine garden plants. They are evergreen and grow best in moist, acidic soils in a position with some shelter and protection.

Blechnum spicant is a British native from sheltered woodlands. As such it grows well under shrubs and trees, also in walls and on old tree stumps, conditions easily replicated in the garden creating a charming feature. The fronds are long and narrow and rather shiny, and in time it forms a substantial clump. The fertile fronds which bear the spores are taller and thinner.

Quite different is the magnificent Chilean species, *B. chilense*, a huge plant with tough, arching fronds reaching 1m (3ft) in height in good conditions. It spreads slowly from a creeping rootstock and really is best in a well drained acidic soil, although it will survive in slightly alkaline areas if plenty of well-rotted manure is regularly applied. This plant is rather tender and needs a sheltered spot; cover the roots with a thick mulch over winter to ensure its survival. Plant this with Dicksonia,

Blechnum spicant

Blechnum chilense

Acanthus, Fatsia and bamboo for a spectacular sub-tropical effect. *Blechnum chilense* is propagated from pieces of rooted rhizome, removed in spring and potted into gritty compost. Plant out in late summer, or in cold areas over winter under glass and plant out in spring.

soil	Both species grow best in acidic, moisture retentive soil with organic matter
watering	Do not let plants dry out, but they need not be kept terribly wet in summer
pruning/ thinning	There are no specific pruning or thinning regimes for this plant, except to restrict spread
general care	*B. chilense* needs a thick winter mulch. In cold winters extra protection like horticultural fleece needed
pests & diseases	Relatively trouble free. There are not usually any problems regarding pests and diseases

	SPRING	SUMMER	AUTUMN	WINTER	height (cm)	spread (cm)	leaf colour	
Blechnum chilense	🌿🌿🌿	🌿🌿🌿	🌿🌿🌿	🌿🌿🌿	80	60	▓	Magnificent evergreen fern worth trying in sheltered spots
B. spicant	🌿🌿🌿	🌿🌿🌿	🌿🌿🌿	🌿🌿🌿	40	30	░	Charming fern, good for banks or in stone walls

🌿 *in leaf*

Brunnera

For attractive foliage and sprays of blue spring flowers, few plants can compete with Brunnera. Easy to grow in shade and happy in almost any soil except the very wettest or driest, this plant is a wonderful addition to any garden. It emerges from the ground in early spring and opens clouds of little blue flowers on 40cm (16in) stems.

The flowers do not last for very long and are not particularly spectacular when single plants are cultivated; instead, grow the plant in small drifts for greater effect. Remove dead flower stems in summer to tidy the plant's appearance. Below, heart-shaped leaves develop, forming good groundcover. Sometimes these leaves feature attractive silver spots in abundance.

Brunnera is ideal grown below shrubs and trees, as it comes from woodland in the wild. It will thrive best in a leafy soil that does not dry right out and looks good with

Brunnera macrophylla 'Jack Frost'

other woodlanders such as epimediums and *Leucojum avestium*. It is perhaps most charming with yellow flowered *Primula vulgaris*. Plants die back in late summer; the dead foliage should be gently pulled from the crown. There are delicate variegated forms that have more exacting requirements, as well as the recently introduced *B. macrophylla* 'Jack Frost'. This is a wonderful selection worth seeking out, as it has lavish silver markings on the large leaves that extend the plant's season of interest considerably. The flowers of this plant are almost of secondary interest. Grow this with black Ophiopogon or dark forms of Ajuga for an interesting combination.

Propagate plants from division of clumps in early spring, or from seed in autumn.

soil	Not fussy, but preferably soil that does not get too dry
watering	Keep plants fairly moist in summer, but do not water-log them
pruning/ thinning	Simply remove faded flower stems, and cut plant to ground in late autumn. Little else is needed
general care	Generally easy to maintain and cultivate. A spring mulch will set the plant off well
pests & diseases	Will get mildew if conditions are too dry, but no other problems regarding pests and diseases

Brunnera macrophylla

	SPRING	SUMMER	AUTUMN	WINTER	height (cm)	spread (cm)	flower/leaf colour	
Brunnera macrophylla	● ●	⌀ ⌀ ⌀	⌀ ⌀		40	60		Charming flower in spring. Bristly leaves are forgettable
B. macrophylla 'Jack Frost'	● ●	⌀ ⌀ ⌀	⌀ ⌀		40	60		This has the added virtue of superb foliage all season

⌀ in leaf   ● flowering

Buxus sempervirens
Box

Cultivated for centuries, box is one of the best-known of all garden plants, mainly thanks to its suitability for low, clipped hedging and topiary. It is easy to please and will thrive on alkaline or acidic soil as long as it is well drained, although plants grow well even in heavy clay soils.

It is hardy (another British native), will take quite dry conditions in summer and is happy in deep shade, although growth slows down considerably. Plants are at the most attractive in spring, as the fresh, bright green new growth comes through, contrasting with the darker, older growth.

The plant is often seen fashioned into balls or spirals and the evergreen, fresh, glossy green foliage has a distinctive smell to it when clipped. Shaped plants can provide an interesting sculptural element, especially in modern, minimalist gardens, where they are popular. Indeed this plant seems to suit

Buxus sempervirens

Buxus sempervirens

soil	Almost any, so long as not waterlogged. Does well on chalk and in clay
watering	Withstands drought, but plant will suffer. Apply water if conditions are bad
pruning/ thinning	Can be clipped into shapes with ease, although plants in shade will grow slower and are apt to be less dense
general care	Easy, if allowed to develop natural habit. No care is required after plants are established
pests & diseases	Box blight will defoliate and even kill the plant, but is seldom an issue. There are no other problems

almost any style of garden. However, left to develop naturally, the plant has a delightful open, slightly drooping habit, which is seldom allowed to develop in cultivation. Naturally, box is an under story plant, growing beneath trees, usually on chalk.

In cultivation, plants will grow well in containers especially if kept well-fed and watered, and clipped specimens can be used to add a touch of formality to a collection of plants in pots.

Camellia

These well-known evergreen spring flowering shrubs need little introduction. They are justly some of the most popular of shrubs for those on acid soil, a prerequisite if they are to succeed in the garden. Most camellias bloom in the spring, although *C. sasanqua* and its cultivars flower during mild spells in the depths of winter.

The greatest enemy of camellias is frost, which often strikes at flowering time, ruining the red, pink, white or even yellow blossom, although more flowers will usually follow. Careful placement is the key in the garden; they must be planted out of early morning sun, which in combination with heavy frost can defoliate and even kill plants. In general, choose somewhere fairly sheltered, such as by a dark, cool wall, as they dislike exposed locations. Plants must have a soil which does not dry out, even in summer, as this is when flowerbuds form; if plants dry out, flowers will fail. Plants will grow best with a regular mulch of organic material. Once established, they need little care.

Usually camellias are grown in association with rhododendrons and other acid soil-loving plants. They can have a slightly 'blobby' look to them, the round flowers dotted all over the plant. The key in the garden is to use camellias with other plants that will extend the period of interest into summer, such as kalmias and crinodendrons.

Camellia 'Jury's Yellow'

There is a vast array of different cultivars; the best way of choosing one is to visit a nursery at flowering time and pick one out. *C. japonica* cultivars are usually said to be hardier than those derived from *C. x williamsii*. Glorious, scented, *C. sasanqua* is a wonderful sight trained against a wall in full bloom during the darkest winter months.

Camellia x williamsii 'Donation'

soil	Plants must have a free draining acid soil which does not dry out
watering	Apply plenty of water in growing season, especially to plants in containers
pruning/ thinning	There is no pruning or thinning regime for Camellias, except to re-size and re-shape them
general care	Mulch plants in spring. If frosts are forecast at flowering time, be prepared to cover plants with fleece
pests & diseases	Aphids and vine weevils cause black deposits on leaves. Yellow marks may be caused by a virus

Camellia x williamsii 'Brigadoon'

Camellia japonica 'Nobilissima'

Camellias are good subjects for pots, provided they are not allowed to dry out, and they may be moved closer to the house when in bloom. Always ensure pots are large enough for these plants.

Remember to use ericaceous compost for camellias and be prepared to protect plants in the coldest conditions, lagging pots with hessian or bubble wrap. You may need to move plants inside overnight at flowering time if frost threatens.

Propagate these plants from semi-ripe or hardwood cuttings taken in mid-summer to autumn. These can be awkward to bring on and may need to be kept in a glasshouse or coldframe in order to ensure their survival throughout the winter.

	SPRING	SUMMER	AUTUMN	WINTER	height (cm)	spread (cm)	flower/leaf colour	
Camellia 'Cornish Snow'					200	150		Small single white flowers early in year
C. japonica 'Bobs Tinse'					120	100		Small rich red flowers starting in early spring
C. japonica 'Nobilissima'					250	200		Large plant with double white flowers early in spring
C. japonica 'Nuccios Jewel'					250	200		Large cultivar, multicoloured double flowers in spring
C. sasanqua					175	200		Species with scented flowers best by sheltered wall.
C. x williamsii 'Donation'					300	300		Popular for spectacular displays of large pink flowers
C. x williamsii 'Brigadoon'					300	300		A refined, large growing cultivar
C. x williamsii 'Jury's Yellow'					175	175		Interesting flowers with yellow centres

in leaf   *flowering*

Cardiocrinum giganteum

Giant Himalayan lily

This extraordinary plant is one for the true enthusiast. It is a bulb, closely related to the lilies and produces large heart-shaped, rather floppy leaves of bright apple green. The plant takes several years to build up enough strength to bloom, but eventually 3m (10ft) high spikes quickly develop from the centre of the plants, upon which are huge, downward pointing tubular blooms of greenish white, with dark red stripes on the throat.

After blooming, the seedpods develop, which are an attractive sight in their own right. Bulbs die after expending all this effort, but offsets are usually produced.

This plant is hard to please. It needs a deep acidic soil, packed with organic matter which never dries out. It also must have good drainage and shelter. The best way to grow it is as a group of several plants, if possible of different ages, to ensure continuity of display. Giant lilies will not easily associate with other plants; they will suffer given too much competition, so they are best enjoyed on their own. Plant bulbs so that the pointed top is level with the soil surface and keep them well watered. Mulch plants annually and watch out for slugs and snails who love this exotic feast. Worse still is the dreaded lily beetle, which will gorge on all parts of the plant from the bulb

Cardiocrinum giganteum

soil	Rich, deep, well drained, acidic and moist. This plant is a tricky customer
watering	Keep plant constantly moist. In winter do not let bulbs get too wet or they will rot
pruning/ thinning	Remove the dead plant after flowering. It will leave quite a gap. Very little else is required
general care	Anything less than ideal conditions and the plant will fail. Plant takes at least five years from seed to flower
pests & diseases	Lily beetle, slugs and snails are the only threat. There are no other problems regarding pests and diseases

upwards. The best propagation method is to raise plants from seed produced after flowering and grow on, planting out when the bulbs are about the size of a golf ball. However, be warned that this will take as long as three years!

Young plants will grow quite well for several years in containers of fertile, acidic compost. This way plants may be well fed and given ideal conditions, speeding up the flowering process. Plant out when individuals have plenty of leaves and have made crowns around 60cm (24in) across.

Carex
Sedge

These grass-like plants have much to offer in the shaded garden, lending elegance with their arching form, and in some cases bright colour. There are many Carex offered in garden centres, but most require sunny positions to grow well.

Look out for *Carex morrowii* 'Evergold', a low growing, evergreen with narrow leaves centred with gold, which is most useful as an accent plant in shady borders, or containers. It is not fussy over soil, and will even take quite dry spots. Conversely *C. elata* 'Aurea' is a plant for damp, even waterlogged soil. The long leaves are bright gold, especially in spring, and make a valuable splash of colour. It will not tolerate drying out and needs more light to colour well than the others.

The toughest of all Carex is the British native, *C. pendula*, a larger plant with clumps of blue-green ridged foliage and arching panicles of brown grass-like flowers in summer. It can be an invasive weed in the wrong spot but used wisely adds a touch of grace to the garden. It looks good arching over water and will grow well in containers, looking especially good in large urns. A pair of these either side of a doorway is most effective and requires little care. *C. pendula* will seed into cracks between paving with ease and can be persuaded to grow in dry shade, although it normally does better in a moister spot.

All Carex are easily propagated by splitting clumps during the spring, and they benefit from a general tidy, removing old, damaged leaves at the same time.

Carex pendula

Carex morrowii 'Evergold'

Carex elata 'Aurea'

soil	*C.elata* must have rich, moist soil. *C. pendula* grows anywhere
watering	*C. elata* needs to be wet. Others tolerate some drought
pruning/ thinning	Remove old flower spikes and any yellowing leaves in spring. Little else is ever required
general care	Generally easy plants to maintain and cultivate. A spring mulch will produce better plants
pests & diseases	Relatively trouble free. There are not many problems in terms of pests and diseases

	SPRING	SUMMER	AUTUMN	WINTER	height (cm)	spread (cm)	leaf colour	
Carex elata 'Aurea'	🍃🍃	🍃🍃🍃	🍃🍃🍃	🍃🍃🍃	60	40		Constant moisture, wonderful foliage. Only for light shade
C.morrowii 'Evergold'	🍃🍃	🍃🍃🍃	🍃🍃🍃	🍃🍃🍃	20	30		Like a spider plant for the garden. Flowers insignificant
C. morrowii 'Fishers Form'	🍃🍃	🍃🍃🍃	🍃🍃🍃	🍃🍃🍃	30	40		Rich green leaves and narrow golden margin
C. pendula	🍃🍃	●●●	🍃🍃🍃	🍃🍃🍃	120	100		Tough, even in dry shade. Problem seeding around too much

🍃 in leaf   ● flowering

Chaerophyllum hirsutum 'Roseum'

Pink cow parsley

This dainty herbaceous plant is seldom seen in gardens, but makes a charming sight in spring. It resembles the common British native, cow parsley, but is smaller and generally more delicate in appearance and has umbels of rose-pink flowers in late spring, held above soft, hairy, pale-green fern-like foliage, at a time when many other flowers are fading, but before the summer performers have started. It does not last for more than a couple of weeks in flower but is well worth cultivating.

C. hirsutum 'Roseum'

It is not particular about soil, so long as it does not dry out, but does best with some added organic matter. This is a fine plant to position close to the front of a shaded border, for although tall, it is so light in stature that plants behind will barely be obscured. It looks well teamed with tulips in very light shade, but in deeper shade will grow with hellebores, epimediums and hostas. It is also lovely with bluebells (Hyacinthoides) in a most natural-looking combination, perhaps in long grass or rough patches under trees. This is another plant that is best grown in drifts, one lone plant has little impact. Once flowering in spring has ended, cut plants back hard to the ground and mulch around the crown with manure, watering well. This way you may get a second flush (all be it reduced) of flowers.

Propagation is by division of clumps in early spring. It is not well suited to cultivation in containers, because it has a rather short season of interest.

Chaerophyllum hirsutum 'Roseum'

soil	Grows best in moist soil with some added organic matter
watering	Plants need extra water in dry spells during summer to keep foliage fresh
pruning/ thinning	Cut down faded flower stems and leaves after flowering; more fresh foliage will appear
general care	Generally easy to maintain and cultivate. As ever, a mulch in spring or autumn is appreciated
pests & diseases	Blackfly can be a problem, as can powdery mildew in dry periods, but there are no other problems

Choisya
Mexican orange blossom

This evergreen shrub is justly popular, having attractive glossy rather aromatic foliage and scented white, star-shaped flowers in spring, sometimes again in late summer. It grows quickly and is tolerant of a wide range of conditions, but it will not withstand very cold, dry or wet sites.

Give Mexican orange blossom some shelter from cold winds, which can cause wind rock in young plants. This evergreen will grow happily in semi-shade, although you will see fewer flowers than those in sun. Plants need little attention, pruning is not often required, if the plant needs to be reduced, the best way to tackle this is to remove individual branches rather than to give a general trim over, which unless done very well can look rather odd. Sometimes a whole branch may die out from the bush, this occurs from time to time and is no cause to panic, simply remove it back to healthy wood.

The form most useful to gardeners who battle with shade is *Choisya ternata* 'Sundance', which has gloriously golden foliage, although in lower light areas this becomes an arguably more easily placed lime-green colour. In fact, in strong sunlight the leaves can often be bleached white, which looks dreadful.

Be careful what you team this plant up with, avoiding bright pink flowers

soil	Plants need well drained soil. Grow in stony ground, even clay, if not too wet
watering	Plants will stand drought once established. Keep them well drained
pruning/ thinning	None required unless a branch dies off, as is prone to happen. Plants can be reduced if outgrow position
general care	Generally, these plants are easy to maintain and cultivate. Plants may be damaged by heavy frost
pests & diseases	Blackfly often infest flower-heads, but there are no other problems in terms of pests and diseases

Choisya ternata

Choisya ternata 'Sundance'

for instance, but otherwise this shrub is a wonderful plant for bringing light to dark areas. It is even more effective when combined with white flowers such as white impatiens. Choisyas grow well in containers.

Propagation of this plant can sometimes be a little tricky. Stems last a long time when cut and inserted into soil, fooling you that they have rooted. Try semi-ripe cuttings in late summer. Choisyas are best planted in spring after the worst weather has passed, to give them time to establish well before the following winter.

Chusquea culeou

The only species commonly encountered of this wonderful genus of South American bamboos is *Chusquea culeou*, a distinctive clump forming bamboo. In time it will make a large clump and grow tall, up to around 5m (16ft), but this bamboo does not have an invasive habit unlike some others; instead of far-questing runners, the plant forms a well behaved clump.

The individual stems (known as culms) are densely furnished with small slender branchlets that in turn bear the small leaves. The whole appearance is rather delicate and resembles that of an erect fox's tail. The culms have a yellow tinge to them and arch outwards when mature, adding to the plant's majestic appearance. This bamboo is not tricky to grow but can be hard and expensive to obtain and is often slow to establish. It is propagated through the removal of a well-rooted culm that should be potted up and established under glass before final planting.

Chusquea does not do well permanently containerized, so plant into the open garden after purchase. It associates well with other tropical-looking plants, in

Chusquea culeou

soil	Not fussy but deserves a good spot. Most impressive ones are in rich moist soil
watering	Will stand a certain amount of dryness, but if foliage starts to suffer, water well
pruning/ thinning	Old culms can be removed to the ground once they look tatty. You may need a saw to do this
general care	An annual dressing of mulch through the crown, with a clearout of old fallen leaves, will improve the plant
pests & diseases	Slugs and snails may damage emerging culms. There are no other problems with pests and diseases

Chusquea culeou

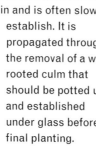

Chusquea culeou

particular tree ferns. Large leaved plants such as bergenias look attractive planted around its base. If you have an open area shaded by trees, try it as a specimen clump on its own where the beauty of its growth habit may be admired. The only downside to chusquea is that, like all bamboos, it is likely to die after flowering, although it may be twenty years or more before that happens!

Clematis

This well-known genus of mostly climbing plants contains a few which will do well in some shade. Most are straightforward to grow and some, such as handsome winter-flowering _C. armandii_ are evergreen, which adds to their value. This splendid species produces masses of hawthorn-scented, white or pink tinted flowers in late winter or early spring. The young leaves are also attractive as they are a wonderful bronze colour.

All climbing clematis are best grown either up trellis work or through an existing shrub, where their large flowers can provide an unexpected contrast to the shrub's flowers, or extend its season of interest. This way of growing clematis is best suited to the

Clematis montana 'Elizabeth'

less vigorous, deciduous kinds which are unlikely to completely overpower the host plant.

If several different clematis are carefully chosen, a succession of flowers can be enjoyed from late winter until mid- to late summer.

soil	Cool, well-drained soil, do best in chalky ground. Will be fine in acid areas
watering	When established are not demanding of water. Should be moist during first season
pruning/ thinning	This is likely to be awkward until you understand the plant's growth cycle. See main text for details
general care	Once pruning is mastered, it's all easy! Responds well to mulch of rotted manure over crowns of plants
pests & diseases	Clematis wilt, slime flux, slugs and snails and blackfly can all cause problems

In spring the spectacular _C. montana_ cultivars are renowned for their spectacular displays of pink or white flowers, even in quite shady gardens. Indeed, there are few

Clematis montana 'Grandiflora'

Clematis montana 'Rubens'

plants with greater flower power.

Propagation is not always easy; cuttings of soft or semi ripe wood (just beginning to become woody) taken in early summer are the most likely to succeed.

One important point to bear in mind is that all clematis should be planted deeply, the soil higher than that in the original pot. This is to guard against Clematis wilt, a disease that will kill all parts of the plant

Clematis montana 'Tetrarose'

Clematis 'Nelly Moser'

Clematis alpina 'Francis Rivers'

above ground. By planting deeply, hopefully, shoots will emerge from below the soil.

Those clematis mentioned in the table below are sure to do well in shade; many others may also flourish. Pruning is a little complex, and is dependant on when the plants flower. *C. armandii* should be pruned if required after flowering in spring, removing any old dead shoots and foliage. *C. alpina* cultivars need similar treatment, and should be trimmed straight after flowering in spring if they are outgrowing their space.

C. montana should only be pruned when it has outgrown its alloted space, again right after flowering has finished. *C.* 'Nelly Moser' and *C.* 'Henryi' should be pruned hard in early spring before new growth starts.

	SPRING	SUMMER	AUTUMN	WINTER	height (cm)	spread (cm)	flower colour	
C.alpina 'Francis Rivers'	● ● 🍃 🍃	🍃 🍃	🍃		200	200		Attractive seed heads. Early to flower
C.alpina 'White Moth'	● ● 🍃 🍃	🍃 🍃	🍃		200	200		As above, but the white flowers show up well in shade
Clematis 'Appleblossom'	● 🍃 🍃 🍃	🍃 🍃 🍃	🍃 🍃 🍃	🍃 🍃 ●	300+	300+		Needs sheltered corner; leaves bronze when young
C. 'Henryi'	🍃 ● ●	● ● 🍃	🍃		200	80		Good candidate for growing through larger shrubs
C. montana	● ● ●	● 🍃 🍃	🍃		500+	500+		Needs lots of space; good for hiding eyesores such as sheds
C. montana 'Elizabeth'	● ● ●	● 🍃 🍃	🍃		500+	500+		Large, scented flowers
C. montana var. *grandiflora*	● ● ●	● 🍃 🍃	🍃		500 +	500+		Flowers are large and ideal for shade
C. montana 'Pink Perfection'	● ● ●	● 🍃 🍃	🍃		500 +	500 +		Large, scented flowers
C. montana var. *rubens*	● ● ●	● 🍃 🍃	🍃		500 +	500 +		More attractive foliage and better coloured flowers
C. montana 'Tetrarose'	● ● ●	🍃 🍃 🍃	🍃		500+	500+		Best for a large space with big flowers and rampant growth
C. montana var. *willsonii*	🍃 ● ●	● ● 🍃	🍃		500 +	500 +		Flowers a little later than the others
C. 'Nelly Moser'	● ● ●	● ● 🍃	🍃		500 +	500 +		Flowers are best in shade, as they will fade in sun

🍃 *in leaf*   ● *flowering*

Convallaria
Lily of the valley

This popular cottage garden plant is renowned for the heady scent of its spires of white, bell-shaped flowers that appear in late spring. Although often seen in old gardens, it is not always easy to get established and seems to do best in light shade rather than in really dark spots.

When it is happy it can become rampant ground cover, spreading via underground roots. The foliage is quietly attractive and persists long after the flowers have faded. This plant is worth growing even if you mean to pick the flowers and put them inside in a vase. A few sprays are enough to scent a whole room. Out in the garden, it is best growing seen through other ground cover plants, but they need to be tough; those such as *Lysimachia nummularia*, Epimedium or even prostrate conifers are suitable. The plant is easily propagated by lifting the running roots. They are generally best transplanted in the green (i.e. when still in leaf) rather than when dormant, so

Convallaria majalis

soil	Not fussy, but avoid heavy wet clay or waterlogged spots. Add organic matter
watering	Keep moist early on, but takes some drought, especially later in season
pruning/ thinning	This plant is likely to spread where it is not wanted; simply pull out offending plants
general care	Generally easy to maintain and cultivate, because it requires no extra attention and tends to look after itself
pests & diseases	Slugs and snails will have a nibble, but not a big problem. There are no other obvious threats

when buying plants, look out for specimens grown in pots rather than the bunches of bare rooted crowns. If you do buy these, ensure that they are fresh and have been kept in moist peat. It is worth potting them up and growing on for a while in a cold frame if possible. The pink form is much less invasive but not often seen for sale. It is slightly smaller with delicate flowers of a light rose-pink. Sometimes desirable gold variegated forms are seen.

	SPRING	SUMMER	AUTUMN	WINTER	height (cm)	spread (cm)	flower/leaf colour	
Convallaria majalis	🍃🍃 ✺	🍃🍃🍃	🍃		20	30	▢	Short flowering period, but superb perfume
C. majalis 'Rosea'	🍃🍃 ✺	🍃🍃🍃	🍃		15	25	▣	Needs more pampering to get going

 🍃 in leaf ✺ flowering

Cornus
Dogwood

A large and varied genus containing trees, lowly ground cover species and most sizes of plant in between, some Cornus are of great garden value. Probably the most popular are those grown for the winter colour of their stems. Many of these will survive in light shade, although the less sun they receive, the less intense the stem colour becomes.

These plants associate well with other winter interest subjects such as hellebores and early flowering bulbs. The darker-

soil	Like moist soil, but well drained. In general, avoid shallow chalky soils
watering	Keep plants moist at all times – most hate drying out. Do not waterlog
pruning/ thinning	Those grown for winter should be grown as coppice, one third of stems removed to ground in spring
general care	Generally easy to maintain and cultivate. Application of a mulch will help, especially in drier areas
pests & diseases	Relatively trouble free. There are no problems in terms of pests and diseases

Cornus alba
'Elegantissima'

Cornus alba 'Sibirica'

Cornus controversa 'Variegata'

stemmed types make an admirable combination with the white trunks of silver birch. *Cornus mas* is a valuable early spring flowering shrub or small tree, ideal for planting under tree canopies. Early in spring, small rounded flowerheads of acid-yellow flowers appear before the leaves are produced. The amazing *C. controversa* 'Variegata' is an outstanding small tree for foliage effect, its tiered branches and white-edged leaves combining to great effect. Its common name of 'Wedding cake tree' gives some idea of its appearance. This is best given some space for its impressive form to develop unhindered, but it may be underplanted with woodland plants such as ferns and epimediums when mature.

	SPRING	SUMMER	AUTUMN	WINTER	height (cm)	spread (cm)	flower/leaf colour	
Cornus alba 'Aurea'	🍃🍃	🍃🍃🍃	🍃🍃	☀	120	100		Golden leaves which stand out in shade; red stems
C. alba 'Elegantissima'	🍃🍃	🍃🍃🍃	🍃🍃		120	100		Fine variegated foliage, good in shade; red stems
C. alba 'Kesselringii'	🍃🍃	🍃🍃🍃	🍃🍃		120	100		Rather sombre. Purple stems, use sparingly
C. alba 'Sibirica'	🍃🍃	🍃🍃🍃	🍃🍃		120	100		Great for red stems, and when foliage emerges
C. canadensis	🍃☀	☀🍃🍃	🍃🍃		250	60		For moist acid soil. Dark red leaves in autumn
C. controversa 'Variegata'	☀	🍃🍃🍃	🍃🍃		450	300		Silver-edged leaves. Slow to establish
C. mas	☀🍃	🍃🍃🍃	🍃🍃		350	350		Wonderful in early spring. Gold-leaved form

🍃 in leaf   ☀ flowering

Corylopsis

A genus of charming woodland dwelling shrubs from the Far East related to Hamamelis, with dangling catkins of pale, delicately scented, bell-shaped yellow flowers in the spring, and soft green foliage during summer.

These oval, pleated leaves are similar to the foliage of the common hazel and appear only after the flowers have faded. They are only really suitable in areas with moist, humus rich, neutral-acid soil. Most need plenty of space, assuming tree-like proportions with age.

Corylopsis can be easily damaged by late frosts, especially when flowers and young leaves are appearing, but plants usually recover. If you have the correct conditions they are easy to grow, but don't bother with them in containers, as they will not flourish for long because they dislike being restricted. They also hate exposed spots, the leaves turning brown if they receive too much drying wind, so grow them under trees and with other woodland plants that like similar conditions.

If you have a small garden the best species to try is *Corylopsis pauciflora*, which develops into a low, spreading shrub with short catkins of very pale yellow flowers. Try planting it with blue-flowered Brunnera or even Myosotis for

Corylopsis sinensis

soil	Moist, humus rich and preferably acidic. Can tolerate neutral or alkaline
watering	Never allow plants to dry out, particularly when establishing
pruning/ thinning	There are no pruning regimes for this plant, except to re-shape and re-size if necessary
general care	Protect young plants from late spring frosts if forecast, and give a good mulch of manure every year
pests & diseases	Relatively trouble free. There are not usually any problems in terms of pests and diseases

an attractive but simple display. It does, however, insist on an acid soil.

These plants in general are not terribly exciting out of flower, so it is best to associate them with plants that will provide some continuity of display into the summer. Propagate from softwood cuttings taken in the spring.

Corylopsis pauciflora

	SPRING	SUMMER	AUTUMN	WINTER	height (cm)	spread (cm)	flower/leaf colour	
Corylopsis pauciflora	● ●	𝒪 𝒪 𝒪 𝒪			150	200		One of the smaller species, but must have an acid soil
C. sinensis	● ●	𝒪 𝒪 𝒪 𝒪			120	200		Larger. Tree-like with age, it is an impressive sight in flower

𝒪 in leaf   ● flowering

Crinodendron
Lantern tree

Once known as Tricuspidaria, these choice, rather tender Chilean evergreens are highly desirable garden plants, but do have fairly exacting requirements that must be met in order for them to thrive. However, well-grown examples are spectacular and well worth a little extra effort.

The most often seen species is *Crinodendron hookerianum*, with its wonderful dangling flowers of bright red in late spring and early summer. These blooms are rather strange up close, as they are fleshy, ribbed and shaped like small eggs. This plant has sparkling, lanceolate dark green leaves that show off the flowers well, and a rather upright growth habit. In fact, plants of both species mentioned here can grow quite tall – even tree-like in time – and will produce great quantities of their elegant lantern-shaped flowers. The flowers start their development the previous year; the little embryonic blooms are thus susceptible to frost.

More unusual and rather less spectacular, but still desirable, is *C. patagua*, which flowers rather later. This species has similar shaped white flowers

soil	Moist, well drained and acidic. Organic matter in leaf mould is appreciated
watering	Never let plants dry out; the leaves will quickly turn brown and fall
pruning/ thinning	These plants should not be pruned, because they generally will not respond well, and do not need it
general care	The hardest time is the first few years before plants are properly established. Mulch regularly with manure
pests & diseases	Relatively trouble free. There are not usually any problems in terms of pests and diseases

Crinodendron hookerianum

and more rounded foliage. When young, it is quite a shrubby plant, but eventually this too becomes upright and tree-like.

Plants are best in a sheltered position and do well against walls; they need well drained acidic soil which never dries out. They may survive well in containers for a few years, as long as they are well watered, but they will eventually outgrow the pot.

Propagation is not terribly easy, although seed that is sometimes produced will germinate fairly freely. Try softwood cuttings taken in the summer. Overwinter on a cool windowsill and plant out resulting young plants in the spring.

	SPRING	SUMMER	AUTUMN	WINTER	height (cm)	spread (cm)	flower/leaf colour	
Crinodendron hookerianum	🍃🍃 ✹	✹ 🍃🍃	🍃🍃	🍃🍃🍃	500+	250	■	The nodding red flowers are set off well by leaves
C. patagua	🍃🍃🍃 🍃	✹ ✹	🍃🍃	🍃🍃🍃	400	200	▯	Not as obvious in bloom, but attractive, with rounded foliage

🍃 *in leaf* ✹ *flowering*

Crocosmia x crocosmiiflora
Montbretia

Although there are many fine hybrids and species in this South African genus of cormous perennials, almost none will grow well in shade, except one: the common old montbretia, a plant that is usually found in most northern hemisphere gardens and is the solution to many a problem area.

Montbretia will grow in terrible dry, rooty soil in deep shade (it will even grow right up beside tree trunks, or in the dry soil next to leyland hedges), producing clumps of attractive pale green, grassy foliage that serves as a fine contrast to more rounded, shrubby plants. It is often seen surviving as a garden cast out beside old hedges and in waste ground; indeed, in some parts of Europe, such as Cornwall in the UK, it has naturalized freely in hedgerows.

In the very poorest of conditions, the late-summer sprays of orange and red flowers are not freely produced, and should be seen as a bonus if they do appear, but in reasonable conditions, these flowers provide valuable late-season colour. This plant makes great ground cover, emerges early in spring and will even survive drought, although the foliage will suffer. In autumn the leaves will die down and can be gently tugged from the corms, coming away freely when it is ready.

Crocosmia x *crocosmiiflora*

soil	Almost any. Organic matter will help encourage lush growth
watering	Plants will be more luxuriant with plenty of water, but do not waterlog
pruning/ thinning	Regular division creates the best clumps. Pruning can also be used to re-shape and re-size
general care	In light shade, flowers are freely produced; in darker areas they are less. Pull out dead leaves in early spring
pests & diseases	Blackfly may infest flower spikes, but there are no other problems regarding pests and diseases

Crocosmia also multiplies quickly, allowing regular division, which means that even large problem areas can be swiftly furnished. Grow it with other reliable shade plants such as *Euphorbia amygdaloides* var. *robbiae*, hellebores, Epimedium and other clump forming, spring flowering plants that need enlivening by the end of summer. Montbretia might be common and unfussy to grow, but it is a real godsend to those with the worst dry shade.

Crocosmia x crocosmiiflora

Cyclamen

The hardy cyclamens are valuable garden plants for gardeners coping with shade, flowering profusely in autumn or spring, and bearing attractive overwintering foliage. These little plants grow from a corm and will seed themselves around when happy. They do best in a moist woodland environment with a well-drained soil full of organic matter, preferably leaf mould.

Cyclamen hederifolium, which flowers in autumn, is the larger species of the two mentioned here, and has particularly fine dark green foliage, marked with silver. Some selections have completely silver leaves. The flowers are varying shades of pink or are white. These jewel-like blooms look wonderful among the richly-coloured fallen leaves of autumn, providing a touch of unseasonable, almost spring-like freshness for weeks.

Grow cyclamens on their own under trees and shrubs, where the leaves make admirable ground cover, or with other plants of a similar stature that will not overshadow them. The white flowered selection looks wonderful with the black leaves of Ophiopogon.

In time, *C. hederifolium* will form tubers the size of saucers, from which many dozens of flowers will emerge.

Spring flowering *C. coum* is rather similar but smaller. The little leaves are heart shaped and usually splashed with silver. As it is smaller, this species is perhaps less well suited for mixing with other plants and does well in slightly brighter areas, light dappled shade suiting it

Cyclamen coum 'Album'

Cyclamen coum

Cyclamen hederifolium

soil	Rich and well drained. Added grit and leafmould at planting time will help
watering	When establishing, do not let dry out. Will tolerate some drought when settled
pruning/ thinning	There are no specific pruning or thinning regimes for this plant, except to re-shape and re-size
general care	A mulch of leaf mould or rotted manure keeps them flourishing. Avoid covering plants with too thick a layer
pests & diseases	Vine weevil will destroy plants by eating the tubers, especially those in containers

well. Plants can also be grown well in shallow pans of gritty compost. Propagate plants from seed, which usually sets on plants and germinates easily.

	SPRING	SUMMER	AUTUMN	WINTER	height (cm)	spread (cm)	flower/leaf colour	
Cyclamen coum	● 🌿 🌿		🌿	🌿 ● ●●	10	15		This dainty species grows well when naturalized in grass
C. hederifolium	🌿 🌿 🌿		● ●● ●● 🌿	🌿 🌿 🌿	15	20		Tougher; will stand deeper shade

🌿 *in leaf* ● *flowering*

Danae racemosa

A strange Asian relative of the lily, *Danae racemosa* is a tough yet refined customer, producing arching sprays of glittering evergreen foliage from a suckering rootstock. The individual leaves are lanceolate, bright green, and very shiny.

Often, after a hot summer, orange berries will appear from the stems in autumn. Eventually this plant will form quite large clumps, the long branches bending outwards. It is a slow growing but easy plant of quiet beauty, but will thrive in quite dense shade as long as the

Danae racemosa

soil	Not fussy, but likes a moist spot with some added organic matter
watering	Will take quite dry positions once established, but do water in times of drought
pruning/ thinning	Remove old branches at ground level after a couple of years, as they will begin to look a little untidy
general care	Generally easy to maintain and cultivate. Simply provide an annual mulch of well rotted manure
pests & diseases	Few, although slugs and snails will attack emerging shoots. There are no other threats

soil is reasonable and not too dry. It will make fine ground cover and looks good spilling over a shaded pathway, or in combination with ferns and other shade loving species. The arching, rather open form of this plant makes it useful as a contrast, especially when grown with other evergreen plants that usually have more upright or rounded outlines, such as Aucuba or Ilex (holly). It is useful indoors, too; cut stems last well in water, making this a desirable plant for flower arrangers, especially in winter. It is surprising given these qualities that this plant is not seen more widely in gardens.

Keep the plant looking healthy by tidying plants once a year, removing fallen leaves from the crowns and cutting out any old sprays of foliage that have started to die off. Mulch around clumps with a good thick layer of well-rotted manure in spring to promote the production of more shoots.

Propagate by division of the clump.

Danae racemosa

Daphne

These most desirable garden shrubs are renowned for their highly scented flowers, often opening in the depths of winter or in early spring to combine well with bulbs and other seasonal flowers. Some species require full sun, while others will thrive in shade, so long as other certain requirements are met.

soil	Soil should be fertile, rich, moist and above all, free draining
watering	Never allow plants to dry out; provide extra water in dry spells
pruning/ thinning	There are no specific pruning or thinning regimes, apart from re-shaping and re-sizing
general care	Keep plants healthy by mulching annually with manure. Prevent other plants encroaching
pests & diseases	Relatively trouble free. There are no particular problems in terms of pests and diseases

These plants do have a reputation for being rather tricky to establish, but once growing well they usually prove to be trouble free. The usual problem is poor drainage, which is essential, and a soil that does not dry out.

Ensure that you buy good quality plants that are likely to be expensive. Most

Daphne bholua 'Jacqueline Postill'

importantly, choose plants that are not pot bound, as these plants hate root disturbance. It is important to find a location where the virtues of these plants can be easily enjoyed. Planted close to a house door, the fragrance can be appreciated when you leave or enter your home; indeed; sometimes when a mature plant is in full flower, the scent can almost be overpowering.

Perhaps one of the most desirable of all garden plants, and until recently very difficult to obtain, is *Daphne bholua* 'Jaqueline Postill', a plant of great refinement. In time it will make a large upright plant with long, elegant usually evergreen leaves. The small star-shaped pink flowers are produced generously in winter and last several weeks, even through quite hard frosts. They bear an intoxicating fragrance.

Daphne odora 'Aureomarginata'

	SPRING	SUMMER	AUTUMN	WINTER	height (cm)	spread (cm)	flower/leaf colour	
Daphne bholua 'Jacqueline Postill'	flowering, in leaf	in leaf	in leaf	flowering	200	200	■	The fragrance is quite remarkable. This is usually evergreen
D. laureola subsp. philippi	in leaf	in leaf	in leaf	flowering	40	60	■	Flowers are hard to spot. Strong fragrance. Good in shade
D. odora 'Aureomarginata'	flowering, in leaf	in leaf	in leaf	in leaf, flowering	120	200	■	The most commonly encountered; superb fragrance

🌿 in leaf   ● flowering

Dicentra

These dainty herbaceous plants are related to poppies and are popular spring flowers. Most are easy to grow, some doing well in shade, so long as they are kept on the moist side and grown in fairly cool conditions. The most often seen is *Dicentra spectabilis*, or bleeding heart, named after the dangling heart shaped flowers of rich pink and white.

The foliage of this plant is attractive and fern-like, adding to the plant's desirability. It emerges from the ground in early spring, when frost may cause some damage to the fleshy, pink-tinted shoots, but in good conditions will make a large plant.

Plants sometimes need some staking if they are large, as the stems are rather brittle and prone to snapping under the plant's own weight, especially after heavy rain or strong winds. The flowers last around a month in total, after which the foliage remains until

Dicentra spectabilis 'Alba'

Dicentra spectabilis

around mid-summer, at which point it usually yellows and can be cut to the ground There is a wonderful all-white form which has leaves of a brighter green.

Smaller but more vigorous *D. formosa* flowers rather later and spreads slowly at the root, making good ground cover under shrubs. The leaves are even more dainty and the small flowers tend to nestle among them. This also dies down by mid-summer.

soil	Cool, fertile with good drainage. Organic matter results in increased size
watering	Do not let plants dry right out until late summer when leaves naturally wither
pruning/ thinning	Remove withered top growth in late summer; there is little else to do with regard to pruning
general care	Easy: simply apply a mulch of rotted manure in spring. Plants sometimes need staking
pests & diseases	Slugs and snails love the succulent shoots as they emerge from the soil, but there are no other problems

	SPRING	SUMMER	AUTUMN	WINTER	height (cm)	spread (cm)	flower/leaf colour	
Dicentra formosa	🌱 ●	● ●	🌱		50	60		Dainty foliage and flowers make this a desirable plant
D. spectabilis	🌱 ●	🌱 🌱			70	50		A striking and easily grown plant in cool shade
D. spectabilis 'Alba'	🌱 ●	🌱 🌱			70	50		Colouring of flowers is well suited to the shaded garden

 in leaf   ● flowering

Dicksonia
Tree fern

The tree ferns are among the most spectacular plants we can grow in this country, and have recently become popular with fashion-conscious garden designers who seem to throw them in to almost every garden they build. However, these noble and often ancient plants should not be taken for granted.

Firstly, dicksonias are often expensive to buy. This is because they have been imported from Australia, as a by-product of the logging industry. Secondly, the trunks take 10 years to grow less than 30cm (12in), so some of the larger specimens are a considerable age. Quite often trunks are offered without roots in a pot. This is because the trunks are actually a huge rhizome and will send out anchoring roots when they are planted. *Dicksonia antarctica* is the biggest species and most often seen, with magnificent 2m- (6ft-) long fronds emerging from the trunk like a huge parasol.

These plants will die if conditions are not correct. They need a rich, well-drained soil that never dries out, in a sheltered corner of the garden. They must be sprayed daily in hot weather and fed regularly with liquid feed. The plants are hardy to about -10°C, so

soil	Rich and well drained. Add plenty of well rotted manure at planting
watering	Masses of water is needed in summer; spray the trunks daily
pruning/ thinning	Remove old, untidy fronds in spring. However, little else is ever usually required in terms of pruning
general care	Apart from watering, apply a liquid feed every couple of weeks for good growth. Mulch annually
pests & diseases	Relatively trouble free. There are not usually any problems in terms of pests and diseases

Dicksonia antarctica

may need protecting in many areas with straw pushed into the crowns where new leaves emerge. Old leaves may be frosted off in cold spells, but new fronds usually emerge from the crown. The larger the plant, the more hardy it will be. Younger plants without trunks are best moved indoors for winter to protect them from frost.

Dicksonia antarctica

	SPRING	SUMMER	AUTUMN	WINTER	height (cm)	spread (cm)	leaf colour	
Dicksonia antarctica	🍃🍃🍃	🍃🍃🍃	🍃🍃🍃	🍃🍃🍃	500	300		Magnificent and best if planted as part of a group
Dicksonia fibrosa	🍃🍃🍃	🍃🍃🍃	🍃🍃🍃	🍃🍃🍃	300	200		Smaller with a thick fibrous trunk. Possibly more hardy

🍃 in leaf

Digitalis
Foxglove

This genus of perennial and biennial plants is often represented in gardens by the British native, *Digitalis purpurea*, a plant that thrives in reasonably moist shade on most soils, sending up 1.5m (5ft) spires of flowers from a basal rosette of soft-textured leaves.

It is a biennial, or at best a short lived perennial, but is easily raised from seed – in fact, it freely seeds around the garden. Usually purple or white flowered, some selections have apricot tones, or flowers whirled around the stem rather than the usual one-sided arrangement. This plant is quite delightful growing through lower ground covering plants such as *Tellima grandiflora*, various ferns, heucheras or even hostas, the spires of flowers providing height and colour.

The white flowered form is superb at bringing light to shady areas, and looks great in front of a dark hedge or in a drift under trees. Indeed you may decide to exclude the purple flowered form from some areas; white flowered seedlings are a brighter green with no red in the foliage and thus easy to spot. A similar plant is *D.* x *mertonensis*, with shorter, squatter flower spikes. The leaves have serrated margins and the blooms are a strange and rather sombre shade of brownish mauve. It makes a better perennial than the common foxglove, but must be regularly divided. Less dramatic in flower perhaps, but neater, and a true perennial is *D. lutea*. This species has little pale yellow flowers up short spikes and long, narrow dark green leaves. It will stand dry soil in quite dark places and is best planted towards the front of beds.

Requiring rather better conditions, in particular more light, is *D. parviflora*, with tall narrow spikes of brown tubular flowers.

For the biggest and best plants sow in summer, prick out into individual containers and protect in a cold frame or a sheltered spot.

Digitalis lutea

Digitalis x mertonensis

Digitalis purpurea

soil	Not fussy. Plants do best in moist ground with plenty of organic matter
watering	If plants dry out the appearance will suffer and flowering is reduced
pruning/ thinning	Remove faded flower spikes of perennial species. However, little else is ever usually required
general care	Generally easy to maintain and cultivate. Mulch in spring, replant seedlings at the same time
pests & diseases	There are few problems with pests, but blackfly may infest flower stems, and slugs and snails damage foliage

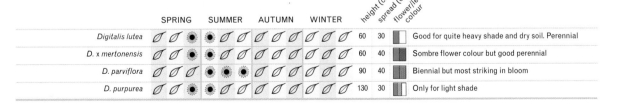

	SPRING	SUMMER	AUTUMN	WINTER	height (cm)	spread (cm)	flower/leaf colour	
Digitalis lutea					60	30		Good for quite heavy shade and dry soil. Perennial
D. x mertonensis					60	40		Sombre flower colour but good perennial
D. parviflora					90	40		Biennial but most striking in bloom
D. purpurea					130	30		Only for light shade

🌿 in leaf   ✹ flowering

Dryopteris
Male fern

Native to Britain, *Dryopteris felix-mas* is perhaps the easiest of all ferns for difficult spots in shade. It will grow in quite dry soil, even under hedges and in dark corners, and seeds around the garden. The clumps of fronds will reach 1m (3ft) high in good soil, and in sheltered sites or mild winters, they are almost evergreen, although the fronds tend to get rather untidy towards the end of winter.

There are many forms of this plant offered with more ornate, crested fronds which may appeal. This is certainly a plant to try if you have failed with others in dry shade, but it is well worth adding manure at planting and mulching well afterwards to get these ferns to perform well. In these tricky locations try them with *Iris foetidissima*, Aucuba, *Euphorbia amygdaloides* var. *robbiae* and *Geranium endressii*.

Rather different is perhaps the most magnificent of fully hardy ferns, *D. wallichiana*, a species from the Far East. In spring the emerging shuttlecocks of fronds are a wonderful chartreuse-green colour and the central stem of the leaf is covered in golden hairs. The handsome fronds become a deeper green as the season progresses and in winter the foliage collapses after the first hard frosts, but is best retained until spring to protect the plant from the worst of the winter weather.

This plant should be grown in rather better conditions; a rich, moist soil with good drainage suits it best. Grow it with choice woodlanders such as Trillium and yellow-flowered *Uvularia grandiflora*.

Dryopteris felix-mas

soil	They do best in a rich well-drained spot. *D. felix-mas* will survive in dry rooty soil
watering	It is best to keep these ferns moist at all times, but without waterlogging them
pruning/ thinning	No pruning is usually required, except to prune into shape or to re-size the ferns
general care	Generally easy to cultivate. Remove old fronds in spring after the worst weather has passed
pests & diseases	Relatively trouble free. There are not usually any problems in terms of pests and diseases

Dryopteris wallichiana

	SPRING	SUMMER	AUTUMN	WINTER	height (cm)	spread (cm)	leaf colour	
Dryopteris felix-mas	🌿🌿	🌿🌿🌿	🌿🌿🌿	🌿	120	100	▨	Tough and easy garden plant
D. wallichiana	🌿🌿	🌿🌿🌿	🌿🌿		70	60	▨	Magnificent species which requires some pampering

🌿 *in leaf*

Elaeagnus

These easy, popular shrubs are versatile candidates for the garden, growing quickly in both sun and shade. Most are dense evergreens (the deciduous kinds grow well only in sun) often with variegated leaves; some also have spiny stems and a rather awkward, angular growth habit. However, they will thrive in a wide range of soil conditions and can be kept well pruned, which is just as well, for they can make very large shrubs if left untouched.

Elaeagnus x *ebbingei* is a plant of considerable merit. It has oval, dark green leaves with silver undersides; the young growth is also silvery, which makes the plant particularly attractive in spring. The surprise comes in autumn, when the plant emits a wonderful fragrance. This can be fairly strong and often hard to place. Investigation reveals small, creamy white, bell shaped flowers, hidden beneath the foliage, which in turn are followed by dangling pink fruits.

The variegated selections *E.* x *ebbingei* 'Gilt Edge' with large, gold margined leaves, and also 'Limelight', which has pale green centres to the leaves, are also well worth growing, especially in shady gardens. Tougher and much coarser, is *E. pungens*.

These plants usually have dark, slightly puckered foliage again with scented

Elaeagnus x *ebbingei* 'Limelight'

soil	Not fussy, will grow in a wide range of soils as long as well drained.
watering	Water well to establish, but established plants will take quite dry conditions
pruning/ thinning	Prune this plant in autumn when it gets too large. Some varieties will make a good hedge
general care	Generally very easy to maintain and cultivate. An annual mulch is all that is required
pests & diseases	Relatively trouble free. There are not usually any problems with pests and diseases

flowers. The golden variegated *E. pungens* 'Maculata' is particularly vigorous and often seen around car parks and as a landscaping plant, for it is tough, quick to mature and easily grown.

Elaeagnus pungens 'Maculata'

	SPRING	SUMMER	AUTUMN	WINTER	height (cm)	spread (cm)	leaf colour	
Elaeagnus x ebbingei	🍃🍃🍃	🍃🍃🍃	●●🍃🍃	🍃🍃🍃	500	500		Attractive for foliage and also white flowers
E. x ebbingei 'Coastal Gold'	🍃🍃🍃	🍃🍃🍃	●●●🍃	🍃🍃🍃	500	500		Fine foliage for shade
E. x ebbingei 'Limelight'	🍃🍃🍃	🍃🍃🍃	●●🍃🍃	🍃🍃🍃	500	500		Subtle and attractive
E. pungens 'Maculata'	🍃🍃🍃	🍃🍃🍃	●●●🍃	🍃🍃🍃	500	500		Vigorous but good at brightening a dark corner

🍃 in leaf   ● flowering

Enkianthus campanulatus

This large Japanese shrub is a good choice for the shaded garden, provided you have a cool moist, acid soil that is well drained, especially in winter. These plants have small, toothed deciduous leaves that are held on reddish tinted shoots.

The leaves turn from green to dramatic shades of yellow, orange and red before falling, and many clusters of little bell shaped flowers, usually tinted with cream or pink, produced from the ends of shoots in the spring. The flowers may be less spectacular than those of the camellias and rhododendrons that these plants are often seen growing with, but they have a refined elegance.

As these plants mature they gradually become more tree-like, reaching around 3m (10ft). This allows one to pass underneath and look up at the flowers. With time, the lower branches become barer, which makes them ideal subjects for underplanting. Foxgloves (Digitalis), hellebores, lilies,

Enkianthus campanulatus

soil	Soil should idealy be cool, moist, well drained and acidic
watering	Plants must be kept well watered. Do not allow them to dry out
pruning/ thinning	No pruning or thinning is required, save the removal of any dead twigs which may appear
general care	Easy to maintain. Give plants a regular spring mulch of well rotted manure or leafmould
pests & diseases	Relatively trouble free. There are not usually any problems in terms of pests and diseases

Enkianthus campanulatus

rhododendrons and Pieris all make fine planting partners. One could even grow a climber such as honeysuckle up these plants for added summer interest at a time when Enkianthus is rather unexciting.

Before planting, which is usually best done in spring, enrich the soil with plenty of leafmould and mulch plants well afterwards to help ensure the ground stays moist. In the first few years the plants will need plenty of water. Plants will grow well in containers for several years, until they get too large. Propagation from cuttings can be difficult, so try layering branches. Seed, if you can get hold of it, is probably the best option.

Epimedium

This large genus of both deciduous and evergreen herbaceous woodland plants contains many of great garden value. Epimediums are, perhaps surprisingly, related to Berberis, and many are equally easy to grow and find a home for in shaded locations. Some make fine ground cover, carpeting bare earth, especially under trees, and the evergreen species do a fine job of suppressing any weeds.

Epimedium pinnatum colchicum

All epimediums are particularly attractive in the spring, with delicate emerging foliage and sprays of charming cup-shaped flowers.

Epimediums are fine plants to use for underplanting larger shrubs, and mix well with Pulmonaria, hellebores and spring bulbs. Most are not particular about soil, so long as it is not too wet or too dry, but they do benefit from a thick mulch of well-rotted manure every year, which should be applied in early spring.

At this time, it is also good practice to cut all down, even evergreen species, just before the new shoots emerge from the ground. However, great care must be taken when doing this, as it is easy to damage the delicate young growth of epimediums at this stage. By removing the old foliage, the yellow, orange, pink, red or white flowers are more easily admired.

Some species of Epimedium also have young growth that is bronze-tinted; many other develop rich autumnal tints. For this reason, they are very much plants for more than one season. Propagate by dividing up large clumps in spring or autumn; these plants have slowly creeping rootstocks. The resulting smaller plants must be re-planted in enriched ground and kept well watered in the first growing season. However, even so these divisions may be slow to establish.

soil	Not fussy, but best in a moist, well drained soil with added organic matter
watering	Plants will stand some dryness when established, but keep them well watered
pruning/ thinning	Little pruning is required. Cut off any old foliage to ground level, especially in early spring
general care	This plant is generally easy to maintain and cultivate. Mulch well in spring after cutting back
pests & diseases	Relatively trouble free. There are not usually any problems regarding pests and diseases

	SPRING	SUMMER	AUTUMN	WINTER	height (cm)	spread (cm)	flower/leaf colour	
Epimedium grandiflorum 'Rose Queen'					30	60		Looks splendid emerging in spring, deciduous
E. perralderianum					30	60		Evergreen and tough, make good ground cover
E. pinnatum colchicum					30	60		Virtually evergreen. Good conspicuous flowers
E. rubrum					30	60		Wonderful emerging foliage. Flowers dull
E. x versicolor 'Sulphureum'					30	100		Good autumnal tints. Masses of lovely blooms
E. x warleyense					50	75		Deciduous, one of the best in flower
E. youngianum 'Niveum'					20	30		Small and delicate, deciduous species

 in leaf　　● flowering

Erythronium
Dog's-tooth
violet

These delightful tuberous-rooted plants are related to lilies and are found in the wild in woodlands. In spring they emerge from the ground and produce short spikes of pendent flowers that are held above large, fleshy green leaves, which are often mottled with purple. These beautiful plants are most desirable in the spring garden and are easily grown when given the correct treatment.

Like most plants from woodland situations Erythroniums must have a cool, moist, fertile soil. It is most important that the tubers do not dry out, even in summer once the foliage has withered and the plant is dormant. To help ensure success, incorporate plenty of leafmould at planting time that will help to keep them cool and moist. Once established, they enjoy an annual mulch of leafmould and will seed around the garden if they are happy.

The best known species is perhaps the British native *Erythronium dens-canis*, that can even be naturalized in rough grass with other wild flowers such as bluebells and wood anemones under trees and shrubs if the conditions are to its liking. It has small flowers of white, pink or purple that dangle above the two blotched basal leaves. Much larger and more spectacular is *E. revolutum*, with pink or white flowers, which look good mixing with other spring flowers such as *Fritillaria meleagris*. There are also some rather more choosy, yellow flowered species which may be attempted if the easier to grow varieties are found to thrive.

soil	Soil should be kept cool, fertile moist and well drained
watering	Never let these plants get too dry, or they will die. Keep them well watered
pruning/ thinning	Pull away faded foliage when it fades in mid summer. Little else is usually required
general care	Apply an annual mulch of leaf mould in spring time. This plant is generally easy to maintain and cultivate
pests & diseases	Lily beetle can attack these plants, and occasionally slugs and snails are also partial to them

Erythronium revolutum

	SPRING	SUMMER	AUTUMN	WINTER	height (cm)	spread (cm)	flower/leaf colour	
Erythronium dens-canis	● ∅ ∅ ∅				13	10	▮▮	Small and charming, seen at best naturalized in rough grass
E. revolutum	● ∅ ∅ ∅				23	13	▮▮	Larger more dramatic version of the above

∅ *in leaf* ● *flowering*

Eucryphia x nymanensis 'Nymansay'

This large shrub or even tree is the most commonly seen in gardens from a genus of spectacular, often evergreen, late summer flowering plants which hail from South America. They are grown for the large, scented white flowers produced towards the end of the season, which makes them of the highest garden value, blooming at a time when many other plants have ended their displays.

These plants will do best when planted with their roots in semi-shade, and their tops eventually in the sun. They enjoy a moist, cool, sheltered spot. *Eucryphia* x *nymanensis* 'Nymansay' is one of the most adaptable and freely available, as it will even grow in soils with some lime, and is reasonably hardy, although plants will suffer in cold regions with severe frosts.

This wonderful plant has glossy dark green leaves with toothed

Eucryphia x nymanensis 'Nymansay'

soil	Fertile and well drained. prefers acid soil, but will tolerate lime if fairly rich
watering 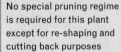	Plants dislike getting too dry, but once mature need little extra water
pruning/ thinning	No special pruning regime is required for this plant except for re-shaping and cutting back purposes
general care	Generally easy to maintain and cultivate. Provide an annual mulch of well rotted manure
pests & diseases	Relatively trouble free. There are not usually any problems in terms of pests and diseases

margins, divided into usually three leaflets, and creamy white cup shaped flowers.

After many years *E.* x *nymanensis* 'Nymansay' may reach 12m (40ft) high and about 6m (20ft) wide, although it is usually smaller. The plant is ideal if you have a garden shaded at a low level, perhaps by trees, as it will grow through the shade to reach brighter light conditions above. Grow it against a dark backdrop, perhaps with camellias and rhododendrons, or else hollies and other plants which will act as a good foil to the blooms at this time of year. Treat plants to an annual mulch and propagate from semi ripe cuttings in late summer, although these are not always easy to root. These plants will not do well in containers.

Euonymus
Spindle

A genus of often large, shrubby evergreen or deciduous plants, usually easily cultivated in gardens. It is the evergreen kinds that are most often seen, as these will put up with a fair amount of neglect and many make good ground cover.

The deciduous species are grown for their autumn displays of berries and coloured leaves, and usually do best in some sun. *Euonymus alatus* will grow in semi shade and has spectacular red leaves before falling in autumn; it is also attractive in spring when the bright green new growth emerges.

Euonymus can all be identified by their peculiar 'winged' stems and are not fussy over soil, as long as it is not waterlogged or bone dry. However, many will stand some drought once established, which makes them suitable candidates for dry shade. Of the evergreen kinds, those most useful to us are ones with variegated leaves that can be used to bring light to dark corners. Of particular merit is *E. japonicus* 'President Gauthier', which is a large-growing cultivar with big oval leaves of white, grey and green. It is most attractive and will brighten a dark corner quickly. Grow it with evergreen ferns, heucheras, box and other dark leaved plants to set off the wonderful variegation. Smaller cultivars can be used to similar effect; there are many different selections in garden centres, some with gold splashed foliage. The evergreen types can be pruned freely to keep them within bounds, and some will even grow as climbers, producing clinging roots from the stems if they are planted next to walls and fences. Many of the smaller evergreen selections are well suited to growing in containers, especially during winter with a selection of other seasonal plants. Propagate from semi-ripe cuttings in summer.

soil	This plant is not fussy at all so long as the soil is not waterlogged
watering	Tolerates dry spells once established. Young plants need water while settling in
pruning/ thinning	Prune plants when they outgrow their allotted space in the garden. They can be trimmed regularly
general care	Generally easy to maintain and cultivate, as these plants need almost no general care
pests & diseases	Relatively trouble free. There are not usually any regular problems regarding pests and diseases

Euonymus fortunei 'Emerald and Gold'

Euonymus japonicus 'President Gauthier'

	SPRING	SUMMER	AUTUMN	WINTER	height (cm)	spread (cm)	leaf colour	
Euonymus alatus	in leaf	in leaf	in leaf		100	200		Magnificent red at the end of the year, dull in summer
E. fortunei 'Emerald and Gold'	in leaf	in leaf	in leaf	in leaf	100	150		Very common as landscaping plant, but tough and effective
E. fortunei 'Silver Queen'	in leaf	in leaf	in leaf	in leaf	120	120		Wonderful variegation
E. japonicus 'President Gauthier'	in leaf	in leaf	in leaf	in leaf	200	150		The best selection for foliage effect

in leaf

Euphorbia
Wood spurge

From this large family of plants there are few species which relish a shaded position, but the wood spurge, *E. amygdaloides*, is a valuable exception to the rule. This plant is seen in gardens in two distinct forms. The best of the two, *E. amygdaloides* 'Purpurea', is a wonderful plant with dusky purple, usually evergreen foliage and typical euphorbia flowers of bright lime green in spring.

It needs some care to do well as it is highly prone to mildew attack if stressed, usually through drying out, and plants are prone to be short-lived. It likes a good deal of organic matter in the soil, but do ensure it is never waterlogged. It will spread around slowly at the root or even set seed.

Use this plant to create sumptuous colour combinations with gold-leaved plants such as *Millium effusum* 'Aureum'. More often seen and far tougher is *E. amygdaloides* var. *robbiae*, an invaluable plant for those on dry shade. With its glossy, oval green leaves and wonderful heads of yellow green flowers in spring, it is one of few plants that will actually spread about in poor, dry, rooty soil under evergreens and by conifer hedges. In better conditions, the roots will quickly spread and it can even become a pest. It is ideal for ground cover on banks or for

Euphorbia amygdaloides 'Purpurea'

soil	Well drained and organic rich. *E. amagdaloides* var. *robbiae* grow anywhere.
watering	The purple leaved form needs constant moisture. *robbiae* stands drought
pruning/ thinning	Remove faded flowerheads in the summer, but there is little else required in terms of pruning and thinning
general care	Generally easy to maintain and clutivate. All that is needed is simply a mulch in spring
pests & diseases	Both are prone to mildew, but *robbiae* only in terrible conditions. There are no other problems

underplanting and is easily propagated by division, although watch for the plants toxic, milky sap to which some people are highly sensitive. Combine with red tulips for a startling display. Plant *E. a.* 'Purpurea' in the spring and *E. a.* var. *robbiae* at any time.

Euphorbia amygdaloides var. robbiae

	SPRING	SUMMER	AUTUMN	WINTER	height (cm)	spread (cm)	flower/leaf colour	
Euphorbia amygdaloides 'Purpurea'					60	60		A delightful purple form
E. amygdaloides var. *robbiae*					30	30		Tough as old boots!

 in leaf   flowering

Fargesia nitida

One of the daintiest of all bamboos, this charming plant is often sold as *Sinarundinaria nitida* or *Arundinaria nitida*. It is hardy and one of the easiest to grow, with small, narrow leaves on slender culms. These culms or stems are an attractive purplish grey in colour adding to the plant's appeal.

This is a bamboo of graceful appearance; in time the culms will form a large arching clump reaching 5m (16ft) tall and as much across if given the chance. It will grow in any well drained but moist soil, but the best plants are found in improved ground and are usually mulched every spring with well rotted manure, which feeds the plant and encourages the tallest culms.

Bamboos can be slow to establish, sitting still for a season or so; this species usually settles in fairly quickly if the ground is to its liking. This plant is not for the deepest shade, but it does add a touch of the orient in areas of semi-shade, and will grow well for a while in a container, which may be useful in areas where there is no open ground or where the soil is full of tree roots.

In the open ground it will spread well via creeping roots, so keep it away from any areas with prized or choice plants. Divide large clumps in late spring to increase the

Fargesia nitida

soil	This plant will survive in any soil as long as it is well drained and not too dry
watering	Water well when first planted. Established plants need little extra watering
pruning/ thinning	Prune out any old culms to let through light and improve plant's general appearance
general care	Mulch with a thick layer of well rotted manure every spring. Remove any old leaves at the same time
pests & diseases	Relatively trouble free. There are not usually any problems regarding pests and diseases

plant. Sometimes the clump lifts itself up from the ground and suffers as the roots get dry. This is a sign that the plant needs dividing. This bamboo grows well as a specimen plant where the graceful appearance of the plant can be admired, or alternatively try it with plants such as acers and hostas to produce a Japanese look.

Fargesia is useful in shade during winter as it is evergreen and usually unblemished during cold weather. Its attractive, elegant form is useful in the garden and contrasts with the upright growth of other plants and is useful for hiding compost heaps or bins.

Fatsia japonica

For instant exotic effect, few plants can better the fatsia, with its large, glossy, hand-shaped evergreen leaves of rich green. It is surprisingly hardy in most areas and will tolerate quite poor, dry soil and atmospheric pollution. It is also quick growing, and even produces mildly attractive heads of creamy white flowers in late autumn, which may be followed by shiny black berries.

This is a plant well suited to city life, growing well in courtyards and looking good near buildings. However, it is worth taking some care over this plant to ensure that it gives of its very best. In poor conditions leaves will be smaller and of a yellowish green. Instead, position it in a warm, sheltered corner and add plenty of organic matter to the soil. In hot, dry periods give it extra water and mulch well with manure every year. This should induce it to produce larger, lusher foliage in spring.

Over the years, old plants may develop bare stems which some dislike, but others feel add to its appeal. The plant can then be underplanted with ferns and other plants to enhance the exotic feel.

Fatsias look good with bamboos and other exotic plants – ideal if you want to create an urban jungle in a shady garden. They will also grow well as specimen plants in large containers. Look out for wonderful variegated selections with white or gold splashed leaves,

although these certainly need extra care and a more sheltered position. Propagate from semi-ripe cuttings taken in the summer.

soil	This plant is not too fussy but avoid waterlogged or very dry soil
watering	Likes to be kept moist, but when established will withstand some drought
pruning/ thinning	There is not specific pruning regme for this plant, except to re-shape and to keep size
general care	Give the plant a decent mulch of manure and wait for larger leaves. Little else is required
pests & diseases	None, but frost can damage emerging leaves in spring as well as the flowers in late autumn

Fatsia japonica

Galanthus
Snowdrop

Ever popular, the snowdrop is often seen as the harbinger of spring; the little nodding white flowers of this bulb gladden even the sternest heart. They are easy plants to grow in most soils, except those that are constantly waterlogged or bone dry, and will spread freely when happy.

Galanthus 'Magnet'

There is a vast range of named selections and cultivars, some of which are hard to keep going and are astonishingly costly to buy. For most purposes it is best to concentrate on those most freely available, as these are likely to bulk up the quickest and will put up with a broader range of conditions.

In general, snowdrops like a cool, moist position in a well-drained soil. They relish the addition of leafmould in to the soil, and in these conditions will quickly form large plants which must be regularly divided to ensure a fine crop of flowers. The common snowdrop, *G. nivalis* and the double form *G. nivalis* 'Flora Plena' are those most often seen and may be bought 'in the green', in spring after flowering, as bulbs with leaves still attached. This is a far better method than buying dry bulbs, as they seldom survive and it really isn't worth planting them. Some of the best named selections are strong enough to do well without too much attention, such as *G.*

Galanthus nivalis

soil	These plants will do best in moist cool, humus-rich conditions
watering	Keep plants moist in growing season, even when dormant. Must not get too dry
pruning/ thinning	Any clumps should be split regularly. Old foliage will die away to nothing. Little else required
general care	Generally easy to maintain and cultivate. Mulch in early spring before flowering, but little else is needed
pests & diseases	Relatively trouble free. There are not usually any problems regarding pests and diseases

'Sam Arnott' with large, well proportioned flowers or *G.* 'Magnet' with flowers hanging on long pedicels (flower stalks).

Propagation is usually best carried out by splitting clumps after flowering. This is actually beneficial, as those clumps that have grown too large and congested actually reduce the number of flowers they produce.

Galanthus 'Sam Arnott'

	SPRING	SUMMER	AUTUMN	WINTER	height (cm)	spread (cm)	flower colour	
Galanthus 'Lady Beatrix Stanley'	● 🍃 🍃 🍃			● ●	15	15	☐	Good reliable double cultivar
G. 'Magnet'	● 🍃 🍃 🍃			● ●	25	25	☐	Large flowers dangle on long pedicels
G. nivalis	● 🍃 🍃 🍃			● ●	15	15	☐	The common snowdrop. Perfect!
G. nivalis 'Flora Plena'	● 🍃 🍃 🍃			● ●	15	15	☐	Double form of above, slightly messy flower
G. 'Sam Arnott'	● 🍃 🍃 🍃			● ●	20	20	☐	Good, strong growing, well shaped single

🍃 in leaf   ● flowering

Plants for Shade

G

Garrya
Tassel bush

With evergreen leaves of a drab grey-green, on large rather graceless bushes, garryas appear quite gloomy for much of the year. That is until the late winter, when they are suddenly transformed by long dangling catkins of tiny pale greenish flowers that sway in the slightest breeze.

These are astonishingly beautiful when looked at up close, and a good crop on a well-grown plant is certainly an arresting sight, especially at this time of year when floral beauty can be rather thin on the ground. Male plants are said to have the longest tassels.

However, these plants are not always easy to keep looking at their best. Despite the coarse appearance, they are actually rather tender and are easily damaged by frosts and cold drying winds. In even average winters they will suffer in cold spells, developing unsightly necrotic patches on the leaves. Garryas are not particular about soil – they even tolerate poor conditions – but it must be well drained. The best solution is to grow them against a shady but sheltered wall, where they will receive protection and can be kept trained to the wall, taking up less space then those freestanding out in the open.

In summer, garryas are best enlivened by for example allowing a clematis to ramble through them, or by planting something bright directly in front, as otherwise they

Garrya elliptica

G

Plants for Shade

soil	No particular type of soil is required, but avoid water-logged sites
watering	Water well when young; established plants will not need extra water
pruning/ thinning	Keep all the plants on walls trimmed to size, and also tie in shoots to the wall
general care	No general care is really required, however the occasional mulch will assist growth
pests & diseases	Not usually any problems with pests and diseases, but winter damage to leaves is unsightly

can look very dull. The cultivar *Garrya elliptica* 'James Roof' is popular for its extra long catkins.

Do not attempt to grow these plants in a container, as they rarely do well. Propagate from semi ripe cuttings in summer.

	SPRING	SUMMER	AUTUMN	WINTER	height (cm)	spread (cm)	flower/leaf colour	
Garrya elliptica					400	400		Best grown on a shady sheltered wall
G. elliptica 'James Roof'					400	400		Extra long catkins

 in leaf   *flowering*

Gaultheria

These members of the heath family (Ericaceae) are grown almost entirely for the beauty of their wonderful berries. *Gaultheria mucronata* is also sold as *Pernettya mucronata*, and is an evergreen, shrubby plant, which spreads by underground suckers. It is usually low and compact in growth, and the small leaves are rather spiny, which makes weeding around these plants an uncomfortable chore.

The flowers appear in early summer and are tiny, white and usually missed, but the shiny berries that are carried by female and hermaphrodite forms make a spectacular splash of colour. There are many named selections with white, pink or red fruits, and it is essential to have at least one male plant to ensure a good crop. While it is wise to associate these plants with others that will flower and provide some interest when the gaultherias are not fruiting, for real impact choose a selection of different coloured fruiting forms and mass them together. Gaultherias are not well suited to growing in containers.

The other commonly seen Gaultheria is *G. procumbens*, a low creeping plant which spreads freely when happy, and has shiny

Gaultheria mucronata

Gaultheria wisleyensis 'Wisley Pearl'

oval leaves and white flowers which are followed by glossy red berries in winter. It makes fine ground cover and is attractive in mixed containers with other seasonal plants such as Skimmia, ivies and winter heathers.

Both these plants need a moist, cool, peaty, acidic soil which is freely drained (they are often best in a slightly sandy soil), and associate well with Pieris and rhododendrons. Propagate plants from rooted suckers.

soil 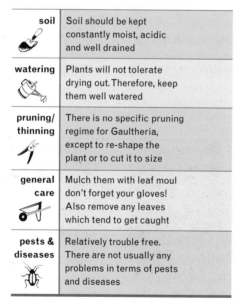	Soil should be kept constantly moist, acidic and well drained
watering	Plants will not tolerate drying out. Therefore, keep them well watered
pruning/ thinning	There is no specific pruning regime for Gaultheria, except to re-shape the plant or to cut it to size
general care	Mulch them with leaf moul don't forget your gloves! Also remove any leaves which tend to get caught
pests & diseases	Relatively trouble free. There are not usually any problems in terms of pests and diseases

	SPRING			SUMMER			AUTUMN			WINTER			height (cm)	spread (cm)	flower/berry colour	
Gaultheria mucronata	🍃	🍃	🍃	🍃	🍃	🍃	🍃	✹	✹	✹	✹	🍃	120	120	▮▮	Spiky. Super berries. Grow *Tropaeolum speciosum* over it
G. procumbens	🍃	🍃	🍃	🍃	🍃	🍃	🍃	🍃	🍃	✹	✹	✹	20	40	▮▮	Best in pots
G. wisleyensis 'Wisley Pearl'	🍃	🍃	🍃	🍃	🍃	🍃	🍃	🍃	✹	✹	✹	✹	30	45	▮▮	White flowers and dark purple-red fruits

🍃 in leaf   ✹ flowering

Geranium

This popular genus of herbaceous plants is of the highest value in the garden, with a huge number of species, selections and cultivars. Most will grow and flower well in some shade, although many will perform best in sun. Geraniums are usually easy to grow and are not generally particular about soil, some thriving in poor dry conditions. However, most appreciate a fertile, well-drained position and will repay an annual mulch of well-rotted manure with increased vigour and flower production.

Geraniums have a long flowering period. Some such as *Geranium phaeum*, which has strange blooms of dark purple, begin early in the season, while others such as the wonderful mauve *G. wallichianum* 'Buxton's Variety' blooms at its close. Those flowering early will often repeat the display later in the year after being cut down and well fed.

Geraniums come in a wide range of flower colours from near black, purple, pink, cerise, blue, rose and white. Some also have coloured foliage to add to the display. Plants need chopping back to ground level in late autumn, although some are almost evergreen in mild winters. Some geraniums will need support; the best and simplest method is to use canes and garden twine to hold flopping clumps together, although this is usually a sign that plants are near the end of their display and need chopping back.

Geraniums are easy to propagate from via seed or most often through division of large clumps; these should be replanted in improved soil and kept well watered until established. Most geraniums are hardy and reliable garden plants.

Geranium phaeum

soil	Some grow in poor, dry soil. Others need moisture and organic matter
watering	If plants are moist they will flower for longer. Some survive in near drought
pruning/ thinning	Cut any clumps to the ground once flowering is complete. Little else is required
general care	Generally easy to maintain and culitvate. Should mulch with well rotted manure in spring
pests & diseases	Relatively trouble free. There are not usually any problems regarding pests and diseases

Some species, such as pink *G. endressii*, are particularly tough and make good flowering ground cover under trees and by hedges in heavy shade and poor dry soil. *G. sylvaticum* 'Mayflower' is wonderful with violet-blue flowers that appear almost to glow, especially at around dusk.

Geranium x oxonianum 'Wargrave Pink'

Geranium sanguineum

Geranium endressii

G. sanguineum is low growing and well suited to the front of beds and borders. Others like *G. palmatum*, with its handsome foliage, need more pampering in a sheltered spot.

Generally, these are not the sort of plants you would wish to grow alone in a pot. They need planting partners to mix with and ramble through. When planted alone it is fair to say that they can look rather a mess.

Use geraniums to knit together planting schemes, threading their stems through plants such as ferns, small shrubs like *Ilex crenata* 'Golden Gem', Euonymus and Skimmia. Cultivars such as *G.* 'Anne Folkard' will climb up through larger shrubs. They can also be used to mask bare lower stems of mature shrubs such as mahonias.

	SPRING	SUMMER	AUTUMN	WINTER	height (cm)	spread (cm)	flower colour	
Geranium 'Anne Folkard'					50	100		Easy, large fine foliage
G. endressii					40	50		Semi evergreen leaves and flowers all summer
G. macrorrhizum					30	50		Low growing, fine ground cover. Tinted leaves in autumn
G. x magnificum					45	60		Wonderful summer display
G. x oxonianum 'Claridge Druce'					70	70		Tough, semi evergreen. Good even in dry shade
G. x oxonianum 'Wargrave Pink'					40	60		Very tough, makes fine ground cover
G. palmatum					60	60		Large rounded leaves, forms low trunk, rather tender
G. phaeum					75	45		Strange flower colour, but endearing plant
G. phaeum 'Samobor'					75	45		Similar to above but with wonderful marked foliage
G. pratense					75	60		Lovely; does best in rich moist soil
G. renardii					30	30		Quite neat; only for light dappled shade
G. sanguineum					30	50		Low growing but tough and easy. Good at front of borders
G. sylvaticum 'Mayflower'					80	50		Lovely for moist shade. Short flowering period
G. wallichianum 'Buxton's Variety'					40	100		Grows stems from a central crown; great late performer

in leaf   flowering

Hakonechloa macra 'Aureola'

This wonderful deciduous grass is a most desirable plant for a decent, moist but well drained, nutrient rich soil in shade. This selection from the plain green species has long, arching leaves of gold and green, produced from a gently creeping roostock.

Once happy, this plant grows fairly easily, but new plants can take a while to establish properly. *Hakonechloa macra* 'Aureola' is superb as an underplanting to shrubs, and mixes in well with ferns and hellebores, adding a splash of colour during summer. It also naturally creates exciting contrasts with dark leaved plants such as some heucheras and selections of Ajuga.

Grown on a cool, wet bank this plant is at its most dramatic, forming a cascade of dripping golden foliage. It produces dainty sprays of little grass flowers in autumn, at which time the leaves often become slightly tinged with pink. Hakonechloa can take a while to establish, but once it has settled properly it grows fairly quickly. The plant emerges from the ground in early spring, at which time it should be given a good thick mulch of manure to power it for the season ahead. In autumn after the first frosts have defoliated it, simply cut any remaining growth away.

Hakonechloa grows well in a container, where its magnificent growth habit can be admired to best effect. Mature plants can

look rather like huge golden fibre optic lamps, and can be used to illuminate dark corners.

Propagate this plant by division of clumps in spring. Do not make the divisions too small, or they will take ages to establish.

soil	Moist, rich and well drained soil. Will take poorer conditions
watering	Keep the plant moist, especially during hot weather. Do not let it dry out
pruning/ thinning	Cut off any old stems and leaves in late autumn. Little else is required regarding pruning and thinning
general care	Generally easy to maintain and cultivate. Provide a mulch of well-rotted manure in spring
pests & diseases	Relatively trouble free. There are not usually any problems in terms of pests and diseases

Hakonechloa macra 'Aureola'

Hamamelis
Witch hazel

These large deciduous shrubs and small trees are perhaps the finest plants for winter effect, producing masses of strange looking spidery flowers which seem impervious to the hardest frosts. They appear from bare branches during the coldest periods of the winter, lifting the spirits of many a gardener.

The flowers are often strongly scented of citrus and spice and come in a range of colours depending on the cultivar chosen, from pale yellow to dark red. The cultivar 'Pallida' is one of the most desirable. Its flowers are the most highly scented and are bright yellow, produced in great quantities. Some others also have attractive autumn tints. After many years they will form an open vase shaped shrub, and it is possible to grow climbers up them for summer interest, with the hazel-like leaves forming a good even backdrop.

Witch hazels are best teamed with other winter flowering plants; try underplanting with snowdrops (Galanthus) or combining with Mahonia and early hellebores. They are generally woodland plants and so like the usual moist, fertile but well drained conditions. They also grow best on acid soil,

Hamamelis x intermedia 'Jelena'

Hamamelis x x intermedia 'Diane'

Hamamelis x intermedia 'Arnold Promise'

soil	Ideally acid and well drained. Will take some lime if moist and well manured
watering	They are woodland plants and will suffer if they get too dry
pruning/ thinning	Remove any suckers from the rootstock. Little else is required regarding pruning and thinning
general care	Generally very easy to maintain and cultivate. All that is needed is a mulch in spring
pests & diseases	Relatively trouble free. There are not usually any problems in terms of pests and diseases

but can be persuaded to tolerate some lime if the soil is kept moist and regularly improved with well-rotted manure. Alternatively, try them in containers in which they should thrive provided they are well fed and watered, until they get too big. This way they can be moved to a prominent place when in flower.

	SPRING	SUMMER	AUTUMN	WINTER	height (cm)	spread (cm)	flower colour	
H x intermedia 'Arnold Promise'	🍃🍃	🍃🍃🍃	🍃🍃🍃		400	400	⬛	Masses of flowers, some fragrance
H. x intermedia 'Diane'	🍃🍃	🍃🍃🍃	🍃🍃🍃		400	400	⬛	Sultry colour to mix with yellow cultivars. Not much scent
H. x intermedia 'Jelena'	🍃🍃	🍃🍃🍃	🍃🍃🍃		400	400	▨	Large flowers with good colour and fine fragrance
H. mollis 'Pallida'	🍃🍃	🍃🍃🍃	🍃🍃🍃		300	250	☐	The best of all, with a super fragrance

🍃 in leaf   ● flowering

Hedera
Ivy

Tough, easy and dependable, ivies have a well-earned reputation for reliability in shade. They can be used to cover walls and eyesores quickly (with no need for trellis). They will also provide excellent evergreen ground cover in the worst possible situations. Additionally, they can be trimmed and pruned regularly, will make fine shrubs if grown from 'arborescent' shoots and will withstand drought and air pollution.

There is also a huge range of ivies to choose from, some of the variegated or large-leaved kinds making a bright and bold contribution to the darkest corners. The brightly variegated selections look great trained up tree trunks, although it is wise to keep them in check by pruning off any shoots that threaten to overtake the whole tree. Some of the most choice forms such as *Hedera helix* 'Buttercup' are rather slower and less simple to get going. These need a little more care and will respond well to a fertile soil and plenty of moisture.

Hedera helix 'Glacier'

Hedera helix 'Goldheart'

Ivy produces two kinds of growth. That most often seen is the type which climbs using roots produced along the stem, and is thin and flexible. The other sort (arborescent) is shrubby and usually found at the top of wherever the plant is growing. If propagated, these shoots make fine, low maintenance shrubs and produce heads of flowers in late autumn, a valuable nectar source for many insects.

Getting ivy to climb a wall to begin with can take a while, there is little you can do except wait for the plant to establish. Ivies also do well in containers.

soil	Not at all fussy, although best with some added organic matter if really poor
watering	Water well to establish, then fine except in the very driest spots
pruning/ thinning	Trim at the end of the season to keep plants within bounds. Little else is required
general care	Generally very easy to maintain and cultivate, as these plants tend to look after themselves
pests & diseases	Relatively trouble free. There are not usually any problems in terms of pests and diseases

	SPRING	SUMMER	AUTUMN	WINTER	height (cm)	spread (cm)	leaf colour	
Hedera canariensis	🌿🌿🌿	🌿🌿🌿	🌿🌿🌿	🌿🌿🌿	600	500		Large leaves and slightly tender
H. helix 'Buttercup'	🌿🌿🌿	🌿🌿🌿	🌿🌿🌿	🌿🌿🌿	200	200		Superb in shade – the gold leaves shine out
H. helix 'Glacier'	🌿🌿🌿	🌿🌿🌿	🌿🌿🌿	🌿🌿🌿	300	200		Common and easy to grow. Makes good ground cover
H. helix 'Goldheart'	🌿🌿🌿	🌿🌿🌿	🌿🌿🌿	🌿🌿🌿	600	300		Eye-catching variegated form
H. helix 'Très Coupe'	🌿🌿🌿	🌿🌿🌿	🌿🌿🌿	🌿🌿🌿	500	300		Strange, elongated leaf

🌿 *in leaf*

Helleborus

Every garden should have hellebores. Most are easy to grow in almost any soil; some producing beautiful flowers during winter and early spring, others displaying fine, often evergreen foliage. Some such as *Helleborus argutifolius* and *H. foetidus* will survive in dry shade, while the popular Lenten rose, *H.* x hybridus will flower for up to four months if given a moist, well drained, fertile soil.

The Lenten rose is a prized garden plant, with flowers in every colour except pure red and blue. Named selections and strains are now freely available, with exquisite blooms of remarkably pure colours, and these should be planted where possible. It is best to keep these seed-raised plants separate from any which are named forms. Plants will grow in containers for a while, but are eventually best in the open ground. To show off the blooms of the Lenten rose, it is wise to remove the overwintering foliage as the new flowers and subsequent flowers emerge from the ground. This also helps to minimize disease.

The Christmas rose, *H. niger* is a slightly trickier customer. It has wonderful open flowers of pure white from December onwards, but often dwindles away three or four years after planting. It seems to like a slightly chalky soil that does not dry out and likes to be mulched with leaf mould.

Helleborus can be planted at anytime, but it is best to buy plants when in flower to ensure they are a good colour.

Helleborus niger

Helleborus foetidus

Helleborus argutifolius

soil	Moist, fertile and well drained soil. *H. argutifolius* tolerates poorer soil
watering	Keep plants moist at all times. *H. argutifolius* and *H. foetidus* take drier positions
pruning/ thinning	Remove faded flower stems at the end of spring. Little else is usually required regarding pruning
general care	These plants are heavy feeders and must have a thick mulch of well rotted manure in spring
pests & diseases	Hellebore aphids infest flowers in late spring. Fungal black spot disease may be a problem

	SPRING	SUMMER	AUTUMN	WINTER	height (cm)	spread (cm)	flower/leaf colour	
Helleborus argutifolius					75	80		Tough and adaptable; will grow in dry shade
H. foetidus					45	45		Good foliage plant for awkward spots
H. x hybridus					50	60		Wonderful flowers in spring. Not for a poor dry spot
H. niger					40	40		Difficult unless you have the correct position

🖋 in leaf   ✺ flowering

Plants for Shade

H

Hemerocallis
Day lily

Usually these sturdy perennials are grown in full sun, but some will succeed in shade in even quite dry conditions when established. They emerge from the ground early in the spring, the young shoots looking attractive among spring bulbs and other seasonal performers.

As the spring passes into summer, these plants make quite large clumps of lush strappy leaves. The flower stalks appear around mid-summer and a succession of large but short-lived tubular flowers are produced in a wide range of colours, although most of those suitable for shade are in hues of yellow or orange. These are ideal for brightening up a dull corner. After the flowers have faded, they can be snapped off the flower stalks, and when all the flowers have finished, cut the stalk down as low as possible. The leaves will continue until autumn when they yellow and die back and may themselves be cut down just above ground level.

These plants are generally easy to grow in any soil, although they enjoy some moisture in the soil and will respond well to an annual mulch of manure as they are heavy feeders. The qualities of their strappy foliage make them a useful contrast among shrubs, and the flowers provide an exotic element. They will not bloom well in deep shade, so a spot in dappled shade suits them well. Day lilies are easily propagated through division of clumps in spring. They have thick, fleshy roots that help them withstand dry conditions and make them easy to establish.

Hemerocallis 'Crimson Pirate'

soil	This plant is not fussy, but add organic matter when planting
watering	Do not allow plants to get too dry until well established
pruning/ thinning	Cut plants to the ground in autumn, remove the flowering stems once blooms have faded in summer
general care	Little general care is needed. Mulch with manure annually, and divide large clumps as required
pests & diseases	Watch for slug and snails on emerging foliage. There are no other problems with pests and diseases

Hemerocallis 'Golden Chimes'

	SPRING	SUMMER	AUTUMN	WINTER	height (cm)	spread (cm)	flower colour	
Hemerocallis altissima	🍂🍂	●●🍂	🍂🍂		150	80	☐	Tall growing species, lovely in the evening
H. 'Crimson Pirate'	🍂🍂	●●🍂	🍂🍂		70	50	■	Flowers are scented
H. 'Golden Chimes'	🍂🍂	●●🍂	🍂🍂		120	80	▨	Lovely orangey trumpets, easy to grow
H. 'Stella d'Oro'	🍂🍂🍂	🍂🍂●●🍂			40	40	▧	Low growing and late flowering

 in leaf   flowering

91

Heuchera

These leafy, evergreen plants have become very popular in recent years, due largely to the explosion of new cultivars developed with seductively coloured leaves in shades of red, purple, green and even orange. In summer, sprays of tiny white flowers often appear, held well above the rounded, usually lightly lobed foliage, but these are generally not particularly eye-catching.

Heuchera 'Chocolate Ruffles'

These plants lend themselves to being used to enhance colour conscious planting, the rich tones contrasting well with golden leaved and variegated plants. *Heuchera* 'Plum Pudding', with its metallic, deep purplish leaves, mixes well with the golden blades of Hakonechloa. During the winter, plants may suffer during the worst weather, and a general tidy in spring is usually advised, removing any old untidy leaves, and applying generous mulch around plants to help them produce lush new foliage.

soil	Needs to be fertile and well drained. Add organic matter when planting
watering	Plants need to be moist but not wet. Established clumps will stand some dry spells
pruning/ thinning	Every few years lift clumps, divide and replant in improved soil. Little else is needed
general care	Easy to maintain and cultivate. Mulch annually and remove old damaged leaves after the winter
pests & diseases	Vine weevil may attack roots of plants, especially in containers. There are no other problems

After a few years, plants develop short stems and tend to lose vigour and their youthful attraction. This is a sign that plants need lifting, splitting and replanting rather deeper than before, in soil that has been improved with manure and some grit added for drainage. Do this in spring and plants should soon recover. This also serves as a means of propagation. Heucheras are not plants for poor dry soil in deep shade. They need some moisture and organic matter in the soil to do well.

Heuchera 'Palace Purple'

	SPRING	SUMMER	AUTUMN	WINTER	height (cm)	spread (cm)	leaf colour	
Heuchera cylindrica 'Green Finch'	in leaf	flowering	in leaf	in leaf	30	80		This one is grown for its tall spikes of flowers
H. 'Bressingham Bronze'	in leaf	flowering	in leaf	in leaf	40	40		Similar to 'Palace Purple' but leaves of a less strong colour
H. 'Chocolate Ruffles'	in leaf	flowering	in leaf	in leaf	40	50		Leaves are a glorious colour with wavy margins
H. 'Cascade Dawn'	flowering	in leaf	in leaf	in leaf	24	24		Brown-red young foliage turns silvery with age
H. 'Palace Purple'	in leaf	flowering	in leaf	in leaf	50	60		Popular and good, ensure you get the correct clone
H. 'Plum Pudding'	in leaf	flowering	in leaf	in leaf	45	50		Superb foliage, healthy looking and easy to keep
H. 'Snow Storm'	in leaf	in leaf	in leaf	in leaf	20	20		Not easy to keep going for long
H. 'Venus'	in leaf	flowering	in leaf	in leaf	40	30		Wonderful new colour, seems quite easy to grow

 in leaf flowering

Plants for Shade

H

Hosta

These well known plants are adored by gardeners who are fond of attractive foliage in the garden, and also by slugs and snails that seemingly prefer hostas to all other plants. There is a vast range of cultivars now available: some have huge leaves, others tiny; some have foliage variegated in almost every possible combination of white, cream or gold; others have pure green or solidly yellow foliage.

These plants mix well with a vast range of other ornamentals, such as ferns, summer flowering primulas and even bamboos, but they will not thrive in deep shade or in poor dry soil. Hostas emerge from the ground in mid-spring from pointed shoots, and it is from this stage that gardeners need to be ready with slug pellets or with other slug and snail repelling methods. Foliage damaged at this stage will be marked for the season. The leaves are at their most lush in early summer, while later in the season heads of attractive, usually lilac tubular flowers are produced on tall stems normally held atop the foliage. These should be

soil	Plant hostas in a rich, moist soil with added organic matter worked into it
watering	Keep plants moist at all times. Do not ever let them dry out
pruning/ thinning	Cut flower stems to the ground once blooms have faded. Remove frosted foliage in autumn
general care	Generally these plants are very easy to maintain and cultivate. All that is needed is an annual mulch
pests & diseases	Slugs and snails, which seemingly gorge themselves on hostas before all other plants

Hosta 'Francis Williams'

removed when the blooms have faded. The leaves will last until autumn, when with the onset of the first hard frosts they melt away, often turning an attractive translucent butter yellow at the end. Grow these plants in good, rich soil that is constantly moist, even wet, although some choice cultivars will need good drainage to thrive. When happy, plants grow quickly and will soon

Hosta 'August Moon'

Hosta 'Sum and Substance'

form large clumps. The slug and snail problem is something that has to be lived with. If you can avoid damage to foliage early in the season when the leaves are at their most attractive, then a few holes and ragged edges late in the year are less upsetting. The best solution is to grow

Hosta fortunei 'Francee'

Hosta 'Halcyon'

Hosta 'Patriot'

plants in containers mulched with grit that deters some slugs.

Propagate plants by division of the crowns in spring. This job is best carried out using an old saw, which avoids causing too much damage to emerging shoots. Mulch plants with a thick layer of manure in spring to help feed and keep plants moist during the growing season.

	SPRING	SUMMER	AUTUMN	WINTER	height (cm)	spread (cm)	leaf colour	
Hosta 'August Moon'	🍃 🍃 🍃	✹ 🍃	🍃 🍃		70	60		One of the best gold hostas
H. 'Devon Green'	🍃 🍃 🍃	✹ ✹	🍃 🍃		30	30		Makes a good contrast to more brightly coloured selections
Hosta fortunei 'Albomarginata'	🍃 🍃 🍃	✹ ✹	🍃 🍃		35	30		Easy and tough; a good choice for a pot
H. fortunei 'Francee'	🍃 🍃 🍃	✹ ✹	✹ 🍃		40	40		Easy and tough plant
H. 'Francis Williams'	🍃 🍃 🍃	✹ ✹	🍃 🍃		80	60		Large puckered leaves form a large mound
H. 'Halcyon'	🍃 🍃 🍃	🍃 ✹	🍃 🍃		30	30		Excellent glaucous foliage colours. Best in shade
H. 'Jade Cascade'	🍃 🍃	✹ ✹ 🍃	🍃 🍃		70	50		Large green arching leaves. Flowers early
H. 'June'	🍃 🍃 🍃	✹ ✹	🍃 🍃		60	40		Forms a magnificent plant with large leaves
H. 'Patriot'	🍃 🍃 🍃	✹ ✹	🍃 🍃		50	40		Lush foliage with strong variegation
H. 'Sum and Substance'	🍃 🍃 🍃	✹ ✹	🍃 🍃		90	80		Huge leaves and quite easy to grow. Excellent plant

🍃 in leaf   ✹ flowering

Hydrangea

Think of hydrangeas and the chances are you will probably visualize the large mop headed cultivars with blue or pink flowers held above leafy bushes once popular and widely planted in front gardens. In fact, this genus of usually deciduous shrubby plants has much more to offer the gardener.

Some hydrangeas have more open heads of flowers held above elegant, softly hairy foliage; some have large and wonderfully variegated leaves, others distinctive, notched leaves that turn spectacular shades of red and purple before falling.

soil	Plant in a moist but well drained soil improved with organic matter
watering	Plants dislike very dry positions, and must be moist while establishing
pruning/ thinning	Remove old or dead branches in spring. Retain dead flowers until the end of winter to protect buds
general care	Generally easy to maintain and cultivate. All that is needed is a mulch every year with well-rotted manure
pests & diseases	Relatively trouble free. There are not usually any problems in terms of pests and diseases

These shrubs deserve to be well treated. Give them a sheltered corner that is constantly moist but never waterlogged, and improve the soil well before planting with organic matter.

Hydrangeas grow well under large trees with other woodland plants and are valuable in the garden due to their late flowering habits. One slight drawback is that they take a while to come into leaf, although even then, young emerging shoots may be damaged by late frosts, especially in cold regions. The mopheads, which are still seen in many gardens, need an acidic soil to produce blue flowers; in alkaline conditions blooms will be pink.

There are other hydrangeas apart from the mopheads. *Hydrangea aspera* Villosa Group eventually makes a large shrub. It has long, purple-tinged leaves that are hairy and in late summer, flat heads of mauve flowers appear. *H. macrophylla* 'Nigra' is grown for the winter beauty of its black stems.

One of the finest of all hydrangeas in the garden is the wonderful *H. quercifolia*. It

Hydrangea macrophylla 'Ayesha'

has spectacular foliage that looks rather like huge oak leaves and long panicles of white flowers. In autumn the leaves display wonderful russet tints.

Popular as a climbing plant is *Hydrangea petiolaris*. This useful plant will grow well on shady, north facing walls,

Hydrangea macrophylla

Hydrangea macrophylla 'Lanarth White'

and has self-clinging stems that require no trellis. The oval green leaves emerge from the stems in spring and, in summer, flat heads of white flowers appear. It is easy to grow although plants may take a while to establish.

The flowerheads of hydrangeas are usually composed of both tiny fertile flowers and the more conspicuous sterile flowers that are actually enlarged sepals.

Hydrangeas may do well for a while in containers as long as they are kept well fed and watered.

Propagate these plants from softwood cuttings in summer.

	SPRING	SUMMER	AUTUMN	WINTER	height (cm)	spread (cm)	flower colour	
Hydrangea aspera Villosa Group	🍃🍃🍃	✹✹✹	✹✹🍃		300	300	▨	Wonderful large growing species requiring plenty of space
H. macrophylla 'Ayesha'	🍃🍃🍃	✹✹✹	🍃🍃🍃		150	150	▯	Very free flowering mophead type. Flowers have a light scent
H. macrophylla 'Lanarth White'	🍃🍃🍃	✹✹✹	🍃🍃🍃		120	120	▯	One of the best white flowered hydrangeas. Lacecap
H. macrophylla 'Mariesii Perfecta'	🍃🍃🍃	✹✹✹	🍃🍃🍃		150	150	▯	Wonderful lacecap type flowers. Long flowering period
H. macrophylla 'Nigra'	🍃🍃🍃	🍃🍃🍃	✹✹✹		100	120	▨	Grown really for its wonderful black stems in winter
H. macrophylla 'Quadricolor'	🍃🍃🍃	✹✹✹	🍃🍃🍃		120	120	▥	Superb for green, white, yellow, pink foliage effect
H. paniculata 'Kyushu'	🍃🍃🍃	✹✹✹	🍃🍃🍃		200	200	▯	Produces nodding panicles of white flowers. Floppy plant
H. petiolaris	🍃🍃🍃	✹✹✹	✹✹🍃		600+	400+	▯	The climbing hydrangea
H. quercifolia	🍃🍃🍃	🍃🍃🍃	🍃🍃🍃		120	120	▯	Grow for its wonderful foliage; red in autumn
H. serrata 'Bluebird'	🍃🍃🍃	✹✹✹	🍃🍃🍃		150	150	▨	Lovely lace cap type flowers; leaves good in autumn
H. serrata 'Preziosa'	🍃🍃	✹✹✹	✹✹🍃		100	100	▨	Red flowers; good autumn colour on compact plant

 🍃 in leaf   ✹ flowering

Ilex
Holly

Well-known as a Christmas decoration, holly has many qualities that make it worth enjoying in the garden at other times of the year. Many species are evergreen and produce clusters of conspicuous berries during the winter, which are usually red or yellow. There are also some selections with wonderful variegated foliage.

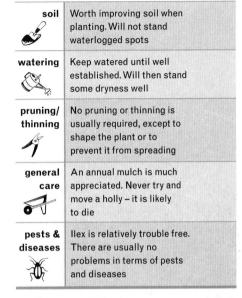

Holly is known for its spiny leaves that make it a fine, burglar-proof hedging plant, although these prickles make weeding around plants uncomfortable work without gloves. Thankfully, some cultivars such as *I. aquifolium* 'J. C. Van Tol' are almost spine free. These hardy plants will tolerate quite deep shade and eventually take dry conditions, although they need plenty of water to establish. Cultivars such as *I. aquifolium* 'Silver Queen' provide an illuminating presence in shade and will look good as a specimen plant with other evergreens, as well as ferns and even hellebores.

If you are growing hollies for berries, remember that there are male and female plants, and for a good crop you will usually need a plant of each. However, there are some cultivars which do not require cross-fertilization to fruit. Holly can be pruned without worry, as they will re-grow quickly, but

soil	Worth improving soil when planting. Will not stand waterlogged spots
watering	Keep watered until well established. Will then stand some dryness well
pruning/ thinning	No pruning or thinning is usually required, except to shape the plant or to prevent it from spreading
general care	An annual mulch is much appreciated. Never try and move a holly – it is likely to die
pests & diseases	Ilex is relatively trouble free. There are usually no problems in terms of pests and diseases

Ilex crenata 'Golden Gem'

they will not tolerate being transplanted. Altogether more compact but fantastic for the small shady garden is *I. crenata* 'Golden Gem', a neat and relatively low growing species that looks more like a box than a holly.

Ilex aquifolium 'J. C. Van Tol'

Ilex x altaclerensis 'Golden King'

	SPRING	SUMMER	AUTUMN	WINTER	height (cm)	spread (cm)	leaf colour	
Ilex crenata 'Golden Gem'	🌿🌿🌿	🌿🌿🌿	🌿🌿🌿	🌿🌿🌿	200	300		Brightens up dark corners. Dense and neat
I. x altaclerensis 'Golden King'	🌿🌿🌿	🌿🌿🌿	🌿🌿🌿	🌿🌿🌿	600	500		Actually a female which produces red berries
I. aquifolium 'J. C. Van Tol'	🌿🌿🌿	🌿🌿🌿	🌿🌿🌿	🌿🌿🌿	600	400		Female, does not need fertilization for berries. Few spines
I. aquifolium 'Silver Queen'	🌿🌿🌿	🌿🌿🌿	🌿🌿🌿	🌿🌿🌿	500	400		Actually a male!

🌿 in leaf

Iris

There are few irises that will do well without growing in full sunlight. However, two species will thrive in shade, although they need rather different conditions. The best known and a British native is _Iris foetidissima_, one of the most useful and undervalued of all garden plants. It will grow almost anywhere, even in the deep, dry shade by conifer hedges.

It has strappy, glossy evergreen foliage that forms neat and elegant, almost architectural clumps of foliage. In winter these leaves will be unblemished by the hardest frosts. Indeed, it is at this time that this plant is most valuable, unusually for its seedheads. These are large and fleshy and carried in clusters, and in winter split open to reveal bright orange seeds. These remain in their split pods until spring, and can be most eye-catching. There are also highly desirable yellow- and even white-fruited selections of this plant. The seedpods follow on from rather sombre flowers of purple, yellow and brown which appear in early summer. This plant is the ideal gap filler for those difficult spots under deciduous shrubs and seeds around the garden when happy. Plants can be split up, but the divisions tend to sulk for a season or so afterwards.

The other species, _I. confusa_, hails from Japan. This is a rather tender plant that will need a very sheltered corner to do well. Fans of strappy leaves are carried aloft on bamboo-like stems. In early summer, lovely sprays of dainty white and mauve flowers appear. Plant it in a rich soil that is well drained but moist and be prepared to protect with fleece if hard frosts threaten. This is a good subject for a pot, as it can be moved indoors in freezing weather. Propagate by division.

As neither of the recommended species are bulbous or rhizomatous types of Iris, they should be planted in the spring as normal.

Iris confusa

Iris confusa

soil	_I. foetidissima_ not fussy; _I. confusa_ needs fertile, moist soil
watering	Both like to be moist, but _I. foetidissima_ will stand dry shade
pruning/ thinning	Remove any old, diseased foliage. No other pruning or thinning is otherwise required
general care	Give these plants a regular mulch of well rotted manure. Generally easy to maintain and cultivate
pests & diseases	The Iris is relatively trouble free. There are no problems regarding pests and diseases

	SPRING	SUMMER	AUTUMN	WINTER	height (cm)	spread (cm)	flower colour	
Iris confusa					70	50		Needs winter protection, but worth the effort
I. foetidissima					60	60		Grow for its berries and fine foliage. Tough as old boots

🖊 in leaf　　● flowering

Jasminum nudiflorum
Winter jasmine

This tough climbing plant is one that every gardener should have the pleasure of owning, and indeed many do. It is grown for the displays of little yellow, tubular flowers that appear from leafless stems throughout the winter months, even during the coldest spells. Hard frost may spoil these blooms, but more buds soon open to replace those that are lost.

By mid-spring, the display is finally over, the small green leaves are produced and the plant is usually forgotten about. It is remarkably long-suffering and easy to grow. True the most blooms appear on plants in sun, but even those in quite deep shade will flower well. It can be trained through trellis, and is usually best grown with another climber that will bloom in summer, such as honeysuckle (Lonicera). Alternatively, let it ramble through other shrubs – even conifers. Winter jasmine can also be used planted through ground cover, the stems running across the soil and over other plants; simply plant and leave it to roam. It is perhaps most spectacular grown on slopes, the stems cascading down. This plant will stand almost any type of soil, even poor dry conditions, but it must have free drainage. *Jasminum nudiflorum* really deserves better, though.

When planting add plenty of organic matter and keep well watered in the first season. Thereafter, apply an annual mulch and it should thrive. Plants seem to do well in large containers that allow them to grow

Jasminum nudiflorum

soil	Not at all fussy when not waterlogged. Dig in organic matter when planting
watering	Water well to establish. Will take quite dry spots when established
pruning/ thinning	Remove old stems which are dying back to encourage more to be produced. Little else is usually required
general care	Annual mulch is appreciated. Tie in sprouting stems to trellis if growing as a climber.
pests & diseases	Relatively trouble free. There are not usually any problems with pests and diseases

up walls where there is no planting space at the bottom. Propagate from layered stems that root quickly and easily.

Winter jasmine is a climber that will grow rather well for several years in a container. It is also of slender growth, taking up little space in narrow, shaded passageways, perhaps along the side of a house. Yet it can inject great cheer and hope into the gloomiest months, its green stems studded with flowers of the brightest gold.

99

Kirengeshoma palmata

One of the most desirable of herbaceous plants for shade, the beautiful Japanese *Kirengeshoma palmata* is surprisingly seldom seen and is rarely offered by garden centres, which seems strange; it's well worth seeking out in specialist nurseries. Shoots emerge from the ground in mid-spring and develop quickly.

The leaves are large, pale green and rather vine-like, held on dark stems. The plant is generally upright in form and may reach about 1m (3ft) in height. In late summer the panicles of wonderful flowers appear. These are a delicate shade of yellow, tubular, with a flared mouth and slightly nodding.

Kirengeshoma needs a deep, fertile soil that is ideally acidic and kept constantly moist. Because of its love of moisture, it grows well around the margins of pools and streams, and is most spectacular when seen growing in a small drift. However, plants will also do well in a moist, cool corner in semi-shade. This plant grows well with aconitums, acers, hostas and ferns. Don't bother with it in poorer conditions, the plant will fail, although it is worth a go in a large container, as long as you can give it enough water.

Large specimens may need some extra support, best supplied by bamboo canes and twine. At the end of the season the leaves will fall and shoots can be cut back to the ground. Spread thick mulch over the crowns

soil	Soil should be moist and rich, and for this plant, ideally acidic
watering	Never let this plant dry out. Keep it well watered, but do not waterlog
pruning/ thinning	Cut *Kirengeshoma palmata* to the ground after leaves have fallen in frosts. Nothing else is required
general care	Generally very easy to maintain and cultivate. Mulch annually and provide some support for stems
pests & diseases	Watch for slugs and snails feasting on emerging shoots in spring. There are no other problems

in early spring to encourage plants to perform well the following season.

Propagate the plant by division of simple crowns in spring. Watch out for slug and snail attack as shoots emerge in spring.

Kirengeshoma palmata

Lamium
Dead nettle

These tough ground-covering, semi-evergreen plants are useful for their often-colourful foliage and white, pink or yellow heads of nettle-like flowers that appear in spring and summer. Plants send out horizontal stems that root into the ground as they spread. The leaves are soft and slightly hairy. Some of the most useful cultivars have silver splashed foliage.

By late summer plants can be rather untidy and may need a trim to keep them within bounds. They will grow well even in deep shade and are good for trailing through other plants. The silver ones such as *Lamium maculatum* 'Beacon Silver' look super with blue-leaved hostas. They are fully hardy, but lose most of their leaves in winter by the end of winter, especially if conditions are wet. This is something these plants hate; in colder climates and particularly cold winters, they are likely to die down earlier.

When planting, choose a moist but well-drained position, even adding in extra grit and plenty of organic matter to the soil to ensure their survival. After a few years lamiums can get a little threadbare as ground cover, especially in less than ideal positions. Lift the stems that have rooted and made decent new plants, and replant, discarding old bare stems. This is also the way to propagate plants.

The most rampant species, *Lamium galeobdolen*, with its invasive stems and heads of yellow flowers in early summer, can be tried in drier spots where it may spread about and cover difficult ground.

Lamiums may grow well in containers for a while, especially over the summer when they can be planted with shade tolerant bedding such as busy Lizzies, softening the edges of containers.

soil	Soil should be moist, yet remaining well drained and fertile
watering	Do not let plants get dry or they simply shrivel up and die off. They will rot if too wet
pruning/ thinning	Plants need lifting and replanting in improved soil once clumps get a little untidy
general care	Generally easy to maintain and cultivate. Regular mulching in spring is much appreciated
pests & diseases	Slugs and snails will munch emerging shoots. No other problems with pests and diseases

Lamium maculatum 'White Nancy'

	SPRING	SUMMER	AUTUMN	WINTER	height (cm)	spread (cm)	flower/leaf colour	
Lamium galeobdolen	🍃 🍃 🍃	🍃 ✻ ✻	🍃 🍃 🍃	🍃 🍃	30	500+	▯	Tough; can be invasive
L. maculatum	🍃 🍃 🍃	✻ ✻ ✻	🍃 🍃 🍃	🍃 🍃	20	100	▯	A little weedy, but attractive in a rough area
L. maculatum 'Brecon Silver'	🍃 🍃 🍃	✻ ✻ 🍃	🍃 🍃 🍃	🍃 🍃	20	100	▯	Unusual leaf colour for shade
L. maculatum 'White Nancy'	🍃 🍃 🍃	✻ ✻ 🍃	🍃 🍃 🍃	🍃 🍃	20	100	▯	Unusual leaf colour for shade

🍃 in leaf   ✻ flowering

Leucojum
Snowflake

These elegant bulbs deserve to be better known and much more widely grown. Some need a hot sunny spot, but two of the best will thrive in woodland conditions. Perhaps the most valuable is *Leucojum vernum*, which appears from the ground in late winter with the snowdrops.

It is a larger, more substantial plant than the better known snowdrops, the nodding, crown-shaped, green-tipped, white flowers appearing in pairs at the top of a leafless stem. The foliage emerges from the ground later once the blooms have faded and is rather strappy and a rich glossy green colour.

This plant looks wonderful in drifts planted with hellebores and spring bulbs. The other species flowers rather later, usually in late spring, and is a larger plant, forming clumps of bulbs. The blooms are slightly smaller and bell shaped, but just as attractive, and this time on much taller 30–40 cm (12–15in) high stems that appear with the leaves. The selection 'Gravetye Giant' is

Leucojum avestium

Leucojum avestium

most often seen and is slightly larger than the plain species. Grow these bulbs under rhododendrons and other plants that flower at the same time. The flowers show up well with a dark background, such as at the base of a yew hedge if it is moist enough, or with the fresh green of emerging fern fronds.

These plants grow best in a moist, rich soil and look charming in slightly wild settings, perhaps in rough grass under trees. They are not well suited to life in containers as they are inclined to flop about, especially after flowering. Plant when in leaf, or even in flower, in early spring. Propagation is by division.

soil	Soil should be kept moist. Rich and well drained kinds suit them best
watering	Keep plants well watered while in growth. Can get drier when dormant
pruning/ thinning	No pruning or thinning is required at all for Leucojum, unless to trim back to size if absolutely necessary
general care	An annual mulch keeps them strong and healthy. Little else is required as generally easy to maintain
pests & diseases	Leucojum is relatively trouble free. There are no usual problems regarding pests and diseases

	SPRING	SUMMER	AUTUMN	WINTER	height (cm)	spread (cm)	flower colour	
Leucojum avestium	☀ ☀ 🌿 🌿				45	30	▨	Wonderful in long grass. Flowers for longer than *L. vernum*
L. vernum	☀ 🌿 🌿 🌿			☀	20	20	▢	Great with snowdrops (Galanthus) and hellebores

🌿 *in leaf*	☀ *flowering*

Leucothoe
Rainbow bush

These graceful, usually evergreen shrubs are wonderful plants for the shaded garden, provided they are grown in constantly moist, lime-free soil. The most frequently seen species is *Leucothoe fontanesiana*, which has glossy, long, pointed, rich green leaves held on arching stems.

In winter the foliage sometimes becomes reddish or even purplish, although this is less common in deep shade. In early summer, clusters of small, tubular white flowers appear. More often seen is the popular selection 'Rainbow', with leaves that are marbled with white, pink and green.

This hardy plant is well suited for mixing with other ericaceous plants such as camellias, rhododendrons and Pieris, that have an early season of interest and need pepping up in summer with some attractive foliage. Leucothoes are good for placing in front of rather leggy plants, as they are well furnished with leaves to the ground. They also look effective planted at the foot of a tree. Alternatively, try mixing with grassy leaved plants such as Carex to provide a contrast in both form and colour. These plants are quite neat growing in the garden and need little attention when established. They reach around 1.5m (5ft) when fully grown. Also

soil	For Leucothoe, soil should be moisture retentive, acidic and free draining
watering	Plants like a moist situation at all times. However do not waterlog them
pruning/ thinning	Remove any dead or dying old shoots from inside the shrub. Little else is required for this plant
general care	Generally easy to maintain and cultivate. Mulch annually with manure or leafmould
pests & diseases	Leucothoe is relatively trouble free. There are no usual problems regarding pests and diseases

popular is *L. fontanesiana* 'Scarletta', an excellent garden plant that has bright red leaves and is a rather smaller plant. In winter the leaves intensify in colour.

All these plants grow well in containers, provided the soil does not dry out, and are ideal for filling a shaded corner with colour. Propagate these plants from semi ripe cuttings taken in summer.

Leucothoe fontanesiana 'Rainbow'

	SPRING	SUMMER	AUTUMN	WINTER	height (cm)	spread (cm)	flower/leaf colour	
Leucothoe fontanesiana	in leaf, flowering	flowering, in leaf	in leaf	in leaf	200	300		Good as a backdrop for other showier plants
L. fontanesiana 'Rainbow'	in leaf, flowering	flowering, in leaf	in leaf	in leaf	150m	200		Most attractive foliage plant, good in large container
L. fontanesiana 'Scarletta'	in leaf, flowering	flowering, in leaf	in leaf	in leaf	100	150		Great plant for winter interest

in leaf   flowering

Leycesteria formosa

Easy to grow and attractive at all times of the year, this plant is tough and a good choice for difficult situations in shade. It produces a thicket of hollow, cane-like stems in bright green up to 2m (6ft) in height, which branch out to form a lightly arching shrub. The leaves are large, soft and dark green and are the perfect foil for the dangling racemes of claret-coloured bracts that enclose the whitish pink flowers.

These flowers appear at the end of the summer from the ends of the stems. The attractive, swaying clusters of blooms are later followed by glossy, black berries that germinate easily wherever they fall. In winter most of the leaves drop, but the stems remain an eye-catching colour; in spring, the young foliage is fresh and attractive.

This plant grows best in fertile moist soil, but will survive in poorer conditions and tolerates some drought when established. It will also survive in quite dark spots. There is a desirable selection called 'Golden Lanterns' that has bright yellow foliage, but is otherwise much the same.

This plant looks ravishing dangling over a path at the front of a shaded border. Leycesterias are not really plants for a container – they look a bit scruffy in a pot – but they do make a fine backdrop to other more brightly coloured plants.

Propagate Leycesteria from softwood cuttings in summer, by seed, or even by splitting clumps in autumn. Branches tend to die back a little after winter and need cutting out to the ground, to encourage the production of strong new shoots.

soil	Best in a fertile, well-drained soil. Not fussy over pH
watering	Like a moist position, but will tolerate a little dryness when established
pruning/ thinning	After flowering in late autumn, cut flowered shoots down to strong buds on the stems
general care	Easy; an annual mulch will help protect roots over winter and encourage good growth
pests & diseases	Trouble free. There are not usually any problems in terms of pests and diseases

Leycesteria formosa

Lilium
Lily

These popular bulbs are not always well suited to life in shade, and some of those that are may require rather specialist conditions. Many, however, can make a wonderful contribution. Grow them with shrubs for summer colour, or through other herbaceous plants to enliven ferns or heucheras.

Plant lily bulbs in early autumn or in spring and ensure that plants have good drainage. Mix in plenty of grit to soils that are heavy, even setting the bulbs on a bed of grit if conditions are poor. Lilies like plenty of added organic matter to grow well, so ensure you incorporate this when planting. There are many lilies that can be considered for shade. Included here are three of the most reliable.

L. candidum is the Madonna lily. This lovely bulb will grow well on an alkaline soil, producing scented white trumpets in early summer on stems up to about 1.5m (5ft). It produces some overwintering foliage, but is dormant in late summer. It likes dappled shade rather than a spot in the deepest

Lilium henryi

Lilium martagon

soil	*L. candidum* and *L. henryi* alkaline soil, *L. martagon* acid soil. Organic matter
watering	Lilies like to be kept moist at the root, yet refrain from waterlogging them
pruning/ thinning	Cut back the stems once the foliage has yellowed and withered. Little else is usually required
general care	Generally easy to maintain. Provide an annual much of leaf mould or well-rotted manure
pests & diseases	Slugs and snails damage shoots. Bright red lily beetle eat bulbs above ground. Grey mould affects shoots

shadows. *L. henryi* is another species good for a limey soil. This plant produces orange, black-spotted flowers with reflexed petals held on stems that may reach more than 2m (6ft) tall in good conditions.

For sandy acid soil, *L. martagon* can create a wonderful show. It blooms in summer, the flowers are quite small and pinkish purple or white in colour with dark spots, and held on stems up to 2m (6ft) tall. It spreads freely when happy. Lilies are a great choice for a pot; they will enjoy the good drainage and can be moved to position when about to flower, only to be shifted out of sight once the blooms have faded. Propagate by seed in autumn or by splitting established clumps in spring.

Plants for Shade

	SPRING	SUMMER	AUTUMN	WINTER	height (cm)	spread (cm)	flower colour	
Lilium candidum	🍃🍃🍃	✴✴🍃🍃		🍃🍃🍃	150	40	⬜	Lovely white flowers
Lilium henryi	🍃	🍃🍃🍃✴🍃			250	40	⬛	Good colour, plants can get quite tall in good positions
Lilium martagon	🍃	✴✴🍃🍃	🍃		150	40	◧	Lovely flowers with reflexed petal

🍃 in leaf   ✴ flowering

Liriope muscari

Turf lily

Producing clumps of grassy, evergreen foliage and surviving in deep shade, Liriope is a good hardy plant for a tricky spot, although not very spectacular. Spikes of flowers appear in late summer or autumn in shades of purple or sometimes white, although the deeper the shade, the fewer flowers you will see. These plants are best used in drifts, in combination with other plants, to make the most of their fountain-like form.

Plants for Shade

L

Try them with hellebores, geraniums and other plants of contrasting habit. The tufts of leaves are usually at their glossy best in winter, which adds to their usefulness in the garden.

Liriopes will grow well in containers; they are probably best used in a mixed planter with ivies, ferns and other evergreens. Plants look particularly good growing through gravel, slate chippings, or with cobbles.

Liriope muscari

Liriope will grow best in moist, well-drained soil, rich in organic matter, but will also survive in terrible, dry, rooty soil, although plants grown in spots like this will look pretty untidy and grow very slowly. Plants are propagated from division, but resulting sections often sulk for a year or so after replanting.

It is important to keep clumps looking neat and tidy. In spring, remove old, dead leaves with secateurs and clear away any fallen leaves that often lodge in clumps over winter. There are variegated selections sometimes offered, but these are not usually particularly hardy. They may be worth a try in a sheltered town garden where their bright foliage can be used to good effect.

soil	Not generally fussy, but best in fertile, well drained ground
watering	Moist when establishing. They will tolerate dryness once established
pruning/ thinning	Remove any old brown foliage from the outside of clumps to keep plants looking healthy
general care	Give an annual mulch of manure. Keep plants tidy, removing any fallen leaves that have collected
pests & diseases	Young leaves may be damaged by slugs and snails. There are usually no other problems

Liriope muscari 'John Burch'

Lonicera
Honeysuckle

This genus of plants contains many that are of great use in the garden and indeed some can make an important contribution to a shaded site. These plants are not usually fussy over soil type, as long as it is well drained, although for best growth add organic matter when planting, which is best carried out in spring. Honeysuckles can be divided into two distinct types; the climbers and the shrubby species.

Some of the shrubby species are among the toughest and easiest of all plants for shade. *L. nitida* is particularly well known as a hedging plant, being quick-growing, having tiny evergreen leaves and forming a dense shrub that can be trimmed and cut back almost without care. It will survive even in dry shade, although plants take on a dusty unattractive look. *L. nitida* 'Baggesen's Gold', with bright yellow leaves that turn an attractive lime green in shade is recommended. *L.pileata* is another evergreen, this time with slightly larger leaves and a more horizontal growth habit, forming fine ground cover in time. Deciduous *L. involucrata* is very desirable but not often seen; it has lush-looking soft, hairy leaves and attractive flowers of red and yellow. It will grow even by hedges, but does best with some moisture.

The climbing species are some of the best plants of all for growing on shaded walls and fences, or even for clambering

Lonicera nitida 'Baggesen's Gold'

through trees. Some such as *L. henryi* are evergreen, others like *L. x americana* are deliciously scented, especially at night. One of the most wonderful climbing species, *L. tragophylla*, is a deciduous late summer flowering climber with heads of large yellow flowers, which sadly are not scented. Grow

Lonicera involucrata

soil	Fairly tolerant, all best planted in improved garden soil in well-drained position
watering	Some stand drought well once established; deciduous types will suffer if too dry
pruning/ thinning	Prune climbing species in winter, simply cut back to keep within bounds, or remove old woody growth
general care	Generally easy to maintain and cultivate. Apply an annual mulch for strong healthy growth
pests & diseases	Black fly and powdery mildew may affect the climbing honeysuckles. Few other problems

it up small trees or large shrubs. Also flowering in late summer is *L. periclymenum* 'Serotina' with richly coloured blooms of purple and pink that have a superb scent. *L.japonica* is a rampant evergreen climber with highly fragrant summer flowers that will thrive in poor dry soil and fairly deep shade. It is good for covering ugly fences. Don't try to grow the climbing species in

Lonicera japonica 'Halls Prolific'

Lonicera henryi

containers; they get too big, although the shrubby kinds will do perfectly well in pots.

Propagate honeysuckle plants by semi-ripe cuttings in summer, or by hardwood cuttings in late autumn.

	SPRING	SUMMER	AUTUMN	WINTER	height (cm)	spread (cm)	flower/leaf colour	
Lonicera x americana					600	600		Climbing honeysuckle with wonderful scent
L. henryi					1000	1000		Evergreen climber with elegant foliage. Not showy in bloom
L. involucrata					200	300		Shrubby honeysuckle; attractive flowers and foliage
L. japonica					1000	1000		Rampant evergreen climber. Well-scented flowers
L. japonica 'Halls Prolific'					1000	1000		Bears more flowers than the plain species
L. japonica 'Repens'					1000	1000		Red flushed foliage; just as rampant though
L. nitida 'Baggesen's Gold'					300	300		Tough shrubby evergreen species
L. periclymenum 'Belgica'					600	600		Deciduous climber blooming early and late summer. Scented
L. periclymenum 'Graham Thomas'					800	800		Wonderful scent and long flowering season
L. periclymenum 'Serotina'					600	600		Late flowering climber; good scent
L. pileata					60	200		Shrubby species good for ground cover
L. x tellmaniana					400	400		Lovely bright flowers but no scent
L. tragophylla					600	600		Huge flowers but no scent

in leaf   flowering

Luzula
Woodrush

Most grasses do not do well in shaded gardens, which is a shame, as these plants bring a special feel with their attractive form and long, narrow foliage. Luzulas make a good alternative, coming naturally from woods and forests, where they are adapted to life in shade. They are hardy and easy to care for, requiring little maintenance. These plants like a fairly moist, fertile soil in a well-drained position, but are generally not too fussy.

Luzula nivea, the downy woodrush, is perhaps the most grass-like species of this plant, with long, narrow leaves that have soft, silvery undersides. It forms large clumps and in summer produces attractive heads of white flowers on tall stems. This species grows well by hedges and at the front of shaded

Luzula sylvatica 'Hohe Tatra'

soil	Plants do better with organic matter in soil and do not like poor drainage
watering	Will take some dryness at the root when established, but best to keep moist
pruning/ thinning	Remove old dying foliage to improve general appearance. Little else is required
general care	Apply a mulch of well-rotted manure around plants in spring to ensure good health
pests & diseases	Luzula is relatively trouble free. There are not usually any problems with pests and diseases

borders, making a good edging or even as a groundcover under shrubs.

Luzula sylvatica is rather different from *L. nivea*, with broader leaves of mid-green and a somewhat coarse appearance. It will grow in poor soil and makes effective ground cover. Rather more desirable is its gold leaved

selection *L. sylvatica* 'Hohe Tatra'. This startling plant produces wonderful foliage effects, especially in winter. Team it with purple leaved plants such as Ajuga (bugle), *Euphorbia amygdaloides* 'Purpurea' or *Heuchera* 'Palace Purple' to make the most of its bright foliage. Do improve the soil well when planting and keep in mind that it will not thrive in very deep shade – it only really likes light or dappled shade.

These plants look best planted in the ground but will do well in containers, especially when they are mixed with other plants, as the arching leaves serve to soften the edges of pots.

Propagate luzulas from division of clumps in spring.

	SPRING	SUMMER	AUTUMN	WINTER	height (cm)	spread (cm)	flower/leaf colour	
Luzula nivea	🌿🌿🌿	✹✹🌿	🌿🌿🌿	🌿🌿🌿	60	40	▓	Good substitute for grass in the shaded garden
L. sylvatica	🌿🌿🌿	✹✹🌿	🌿🌿🌿	🌿🌿🌿	60	60	▓	Good ground cover
L. sylvatica 'Hohe Tatra'	🌿🌿🌿	✹✹🌿	🌿🌿🌿	🌿🌿🌿	50	60	▓	Wonderful for providing colour in dappled shade

🌿 in leaf   ✹ flowering

Lysimachia
Creeping Jenny

This genus contains two well known but rather different plants, both good for growing in shade. *Lysimachia nummularia* is creeping Jenny, a ground covering herbaceous plant often seen in cottage gardens. It has small, bright green, oval leaves and runs along the ground, sending out flat stems which root into the soil as it spreads.

In summer small yellow cup-shaped flowers appear. It is really a bit of a weed, but useful in tricky spots, although it dislikes very dry conditions and disintegrates to almost nothing in winter. Rather more garden-worthy is its golden leaved selection, *L. nummularia* 'Aurea', which has foliage of the brightest yellow, a colour retained well in shade. It is a wonderful plant for edging borders and will run under shrubs and other plants, almost highlighting them. Try planting it with black-leaved Ophiopogon for dramatic effect, or use it in hanging baskets where the trailing stems will drip down rather like a golden chandelier, illuminating a shaded wall or corner.

The other commonly seen Lysimachia is *L. punctata*. This plant is an herbaceous species that throws up stems to 70cm (28in) tall in early summer that are studded with

Lysimachia nummularia

soil	Will grow in poor soil, but better with added organic matter. Not fussy over pH
watering	Plants grow better with moisture, but will survive periods of drought
pruning/ thinning	Cut down stems of *L. punctata* once foliage yellows. Little else is usually required
general care	Generally easy to maintain and cultivate. no general care is really ever needed as it tends to look after itself
pests & diseases	Slugs and snails may damage foliage, but there are no other problems with pests and diseases

attractive yellow blooms. These stems seldom require staking. Try growing this easy plant with blue Myosotis. This species is a tough plant, spreading strongly at the roots, and it withstands poor soils and a good degree of neglect, as well as even some drought. It is often seen surviving well in overgrown gardens.

Propagate plants from rooted sections in spring, or divide clumps.

Lysimachia punctata

	SPRING	SUMMER	AUTUMN	WINTER	height (cm)	spread (cm)	flower/leaf colour	
Lysimachia nummularia	🌿🌿	🌿☀️🌿	🌿🌿🌿		5	200	▨	Good but sometimes invasive ground cover
L. nummularia 'Aurea'	🌿🌿	🌿☀️🌿	🌿🌿🌿		5	200	▨	Wonderful foliage plant to use in dramatic plantings
L. punctata	🌿🌿🌿	☀️☀️	🌿🌿🌿		80	60	▨	Easy, tough perennial

🌿 in leaf   ☀️ flowering

Mahonia

These tough, hardy and justly popular evergreen shrubs are some of the best of all garden plants. Most have fine foliage that is often prickly, and many have attractive, scented yellow blooms produced in winter, bringing brightness and perfume into the garden. Some also are of architectural quality, making handsome specimen plants.

They are generally very easy to grow, surviving in almost any soil, even heavy clay, provided it is not waterlogged, and many will withstand some drought when established.

Mahonia japonica

soil	Not fussy. Will even grow in heavy ground as long as it is not waterlogged	
watering	Plants will stand dry spells, but foliage may suffer and plants become leggy	
pruning/ thinning	Cut back leggy stems if required in spring. Little else is usually required regarding pruning	
general care	Easy to maintain. Give plants an occasional mulch to feed plants and ensure good growth	
pests & diseases	*M. aquifolium* sometimes suffers rust and mildew, but there are not usually any problems with pests	

The commonest is *Mahonia aquifolium*, a tough, dark-leaved suckering shrub that produces small candles of yellow blooms in early spring. It is often overlooked, but well-grown plants of this species can be most attractive, especially after a cold winter when the foliage is often deeply bronzed. It makes superb ground cover and will survive well under trees and shrubs, even by conifer hedges. It seeds around freely. Popular *M.* 'Charity' will also grow in shade. A fine large-growing foliage plant with long leaves

Mahonia aquifolium

divided into smaller leaflets, it flowers well in winter, the blooms scented of lily of the valley. There are various other good cultivars worth trying, one of the finest being wonderful *M.* 'Lionel Fortesque', which flowers in late autumn, the blooms held in erect spikes.

The only drawback is that when weeding around beneath these plants, the old leaves are slow to rot, and they are horribly prickly, so gloves are advised.

	SPRING	SUMMER	AUTUMN	WINTER	height (cm)	spread (cm)	flower/leaf colour	
Mahonia aquifolium	flowering leaf	leaf leaf	leaf leaf	leaf flowering	100	150		Tough and easy, the best for dry shade
M. japonica	leaf leaf leaf	leaf leaf leaf	leaf leaf flowering	flowering flowering flowering	200	300		Upright plant with fine foliage and scented winter flowers
M. japonica 'Bealei'	leaf leaf leaf	leaf leaf leaf	leaf leaf leaf	flowering flowering flowering	300	300		Has broader leaflets and shorter spikes of scented flowers
M. x media 'Charity'	flowering leaf leaf	leaf leaf leaf	leaf leaf flowering	flowering flowering flowering	400	400		Reliable and popular; produces many scented flowers
M. x media 'Lionel Fortesque'	leaf leaf leaf	leaf leaf leaf	flowering flowering flowering	flowering flowering leaf	400	400		Fine late-flowering selection
M. x media 'Winter Sun'	flowering leaf leaf	leaf leaf leaf	leaf leaf leaf	leaf flowering flowering	400	400		Flowers in arching racemes

 in leaf   flowering

Matteuccia struthiopteris

Ostrich fern,
Shuttlecock fern

Suitable only for constantly damp conditions, this wonderful fern is one of the most attractive plants in the spring garden. It sends up shuttlecocks of lush, soft green fronds that are almost luminescent in the spring sunshine. It spreads by underground runners and grows quite quickly when happy.

It needs a wet, organic rich soil, and does well along the margins of streams or ponds. If you do not have a stream or pool in the garden, try in a border that is fed with water from the down pipe of a shed or glasshouse, and be prepared to give plants extra water in the summer. This fern responds well to a thick mulch of organic matter, such as well-rotted manure in spring, spread before the delicate new leaves emerge. The individual shuttlecocks can reach up to 1m (3ft) in height in good conditions. It remains attractive all summer, until the first frosts, when the foliage collapses back to the plant's woody base. If the plant has

soil	Must have organic rich soil to really perform well; will grow in some lime
watering	Soil must be constantly moist, and can even be wet. Be careful not to waterlog
pruning/ thinning	Remove old, yellow fronds at end of season. May need controlling when established
general care	Generally easy to maintain and cultivate; simply provide an annual mulch of well-rotted manure
pests & diseases	This plant is generally trouble free and there are no problems in terms of pests and diseases

Matteuccia struthiopteris

produced any of the smaller, rather tough fertile fronds, these endure and may be retained over winter for interest.

Matteuccia associates well with many other plants. Try running it through plants of *Rodgersia podophylla*, which has large jagged bronze leaves, or mix it with the yellow flowers of lovely *Primula florindae*. This fern will not grow well for long in a container, as it has a running rootstock and will not tolerate drying out. It is, however, very easy to propagate; simply detach rooted plantlets in summer.

Matteuccia struthiopteris

Meconopsis

Himalayan poppy
or Welsh poppy

These beautiful plants are often rather tricky to grow unless you can provide the perfect conditions. Many are native to the Himalayas, where they grow in well drained but constantly moist, acidic soil in a cool but sunny climate. This gives an idea of what must be replicated in cultivation. However, if you can get them to grow, you are in for a real treat in your garden.

Delicate, often large, satin-like flowers in dazzling hues of yellow, orange, red and most famously deep azure-blue are produced over the summer months above rosettes of often rather hairy leaves. They grow well in drifts at the feet of rhododendrons, and mix well with summer flowering primulas.

Meconopsis grandis

Many species die after flowering and setting seed; others are good perennials and propagated from division. There is one big exception to the rule, *Meconopsis cambrica*, the Welsh poppy, which is easy to grow and seeds freely around many gardens. If you want to try to grow the others in the garden, it is essential to find a cool spot. They will grow quite well in dappled shade, out of the heat. It may be possible to construct a low raised bed and fill it with gritty ericaceous compost that you then must keep constantly moist.

Hardiness is no problem to most species; it is the summer heat that kills them off. The key in warm dry climates is to treat them all as short-lived plants. If you can grow them from seed and get them to flower, they will set more seed and thus survive. They also quite like humidity and will grow well along streams. They do not do well in pots, as the roots tend to get too hot and dry.

soil	Sandy, acid soil essential, as is good drainage and plenty of organic matter
watering	Never let these plants get too dry; if you do, you will lose them
pruning/ thinning	No pruning or thinning is needed for this plant, except to remove old seed heads if necessary
general care	General care for this plant can be tricky, except in cooler, wetter areas. Mulch with leafmould in spring
pests & diseases	Mildew will strike if it is too hot and dry. Also, slugs and snails will damage young leaves if given the chance

	SPRING	SUMMER	AUTUMN	WINTER	height (cm)	spread (cm)	flower colour	
Meconopsis betonicifolia	leaf, leaf	flowering, leaf, leaf, leaf, leaf			120	40		Perennial species with wonderful flowers on tall stems
M. cambrica	leaf, leaf	flowering, flowering, flowering, flowering, leaf			50	25		The easiest to grow in normal garden conditions
M. grandis	leaf, flowering, flowering	flowering, leaf, leaf			100	60		Not one for dry warm gardens. Will die after flowering
M. nepaulensis	leaf, leaf	flowering, leaf, leaf, leaf	leaf, leaf, leaf	leaf, leaf, leaf	200	80		Leaves covered in golden hairs. Dies after flowering
M. x sheldonii	leaf, leaf, leaf	flowering, leaf, leaf	leaf, leaf		120	60		Perennial; possibly the best blue for garden use

 in leaf   flowering

Milium effusum 'Aureum'

Bowles' golden grass

This spectacular golden-leaved form of the British native wood millet grass is one of very few grasses which actually does particularly well in shade. It is seen at its wonderful best during the spring, when soft tufts of bright golden leaves sprout freely from low-growing clumps. It mingles beautifully with the soft greens of other recently emerged shoots from surrounding plants, highlighting them with its radiance. The dainty flowers are the same golden colour.

As the season progresses, the leaves will gradually become greener. It is in fact a short-lived perennial, but it will seed around the garden quite happily once it is established, so you can remove old, untidy plants without worry if they begin to offend later in the year. Try to allow drifts of plants to develop rather than simply dotting the odd plant here and there, as that can appear rather piecemeal. This plant is at its most lovely in a woodland setting, bringing a real vibrancy to the scene and making the woodland floor a brighter place.

This charming plant mixes well with so many other plants. It is super with Myosotis, *Tellima grandiflora*, grape hyacinths (Muscari), around emerging fern crosiers, with the rounded foliage of blue-leaved hostas, running through dark-leaved heucheras, under planting roses, and many other plants. This grass also works well in mixed containers and can be used almost like a bedding plant; simply rip it out once the colour has faded from the leaves by mid-summer, and pop in a Carex or something else with a similar habit.

soil	*Milium effusum* 'Aureum' is not fussy, but well drained, organic and rich soil is best
watering	Likes a fairly moist soil, but can be quite dry for short periods
pruning/ thinning	Pull out any unwanted plants. No other pruning or thinning is needed for *Milium effusum* 'Aureum'
general care	Generally easy to maintain and cultivate. An annual mulch will help plants grow well
pests & diseases	This plant is relatively trouble free. There are not usually any problems with pests and diseases

Milium effusum 'Aureum'

Myrrhis odorata

Sweet cicely

One of the joys of the British countryside in spring is seeing drifts of Queen Anne's lace (*Anthriscus sylvestris*) in bloom on the roadside, by hedgerows and weaving through woodland margins. But despite the dainty appearance, this well-known plant is far too invasive and coarse for all but the largest or wildest garden.

Happily a rather similar effect can be had with charming *Myrrhis odorata*. Soft and delicate fern-like leaves emerge in the spring and are swiftly topped by flower stems reaching about 60cm (2ft) high, bearing umbels of tiny but lightly scented flowers of yellowish white, which are seen at their best by early summer. This plant is perhaps not one of the most spectacular of all in the garden, but it certainly has a quiet grace and charm. If the flowerheads are left on, it will seed around gently, coming up in random spots and mixing well with other seasonal plants. Try planting it with early geraniums or with foxgloves

Myrrhis odorata

Myrrhis odorata

soil	Soil should be fertile, and moist, well drained conditions are best
watering	Don't let it get too dry, or the plant's appearance is bound to suffer
pruning/ thinning	Cut down the plant after flowering for better foliage. Little else is required for *Myrrhis odorata*
general care	*Myrrhis odorata* is generally easy to care for, an annual mulch is all that is really needed for this plant
pests & diseases	Relatively trouble free. There are not usually any problems regarding pests and diseases

(Digitalis); it looks lovely under a few trees and will help create a woodland feel. By mid-summer the show is over and the plant can be cut back to the ground, when it will soon produce more dainty leaves.

This easy, hardy plant grows well in most soils, so long as it does not get too dry. It also dislikes really dark spots, but will thrive in dappled shade. This is no plant for a container; it simply does not have enough presence. Propagate it by seed.

Ophiopogon planiscapus 'Nigrescens'

A member of the lily family, this fashionable plant is often referred to as a grass due to its long narrow leaves. *Ophiopogon planiscapus* 'Nigrescens' is a remarkable and popular selection for one main reason: it has black foliage. Because of this, the plant is ideal for mixing with other more brightly coloured subjects, both in the garden, and in containers.

Planted on its own *O. planiscapus* 'Nigrescens' makes little impact, the outline blurring with the dark soil beneath, but mix it with golden Lysimachia or with white snowdrops (Galanthus), for example, and it makes a striking contribution.

It is best planted in a well-drained soil with plenty of fine organic matter included. Keep the plant moist and it should bulk up slowly, although it may sit and sulk for a while before settling in. Mature, established clumps need little attention, although a fine mulch of sieved organic matter can be worked through the clump in spring. By summer, small drooping panicles of white, purple-flushed flowers appear, which are swiftly followed by shiny black berries. These often germinate, although many of the seedlings emerge with green rather than black leaves. It is important to pull these out and either discard or plant separately as they may over run otherwise black clumps. Remove the old brown flower stems after the berries have fallen.

This plant looks good and grows well in a wide, shallow pot positioned at eye level where the plants can be better appreciated. Try mulching the top of the pot with pale grit to really set off the foliage.

Propagate plants through removing rooted runners or dividing up large clumps.

soil	Include organic matter when planting in any well drained position
watering	Plants like a moist position, but be careful not to waterlog them
pruning/ thinning	No pruning or thinning is required for this plant, but you should remove old flower stalks
general care	Generally easy to maintan and cultivate. Simply tickle fine organic matter into clumps in spring
pests & diseases	Relatively trouble free. There are not usually any problems in terms of pests and diseases

Ophiopogon planiscapus 'Nigrescens'

Osmanthus

These fine, hardy evergreen shrubs make an excellent addition to the garden, especially if you have areas of dappled shade to fill with plants that provide important structure, even during the winter months. Some species of Osmanthus can be kept clipped and used for topiary or else grown for their displays of scented, usually white, tubular flowers, which generally appear in spring.

These blooms may be followed during the summer by dark blue or black berries. Osmanthus can be used in quite formal planting schemes as an alternative to box or yew, or may find a home in the more natural looking surroundings of a woodland garden.

In summer, try allowing a clematis to scramble over them for a little added interest. Alternatively, use them as a dark backdrop to show off pale coloured flowers or bright golden or silver variegated foliage. Some species will even make effective flowering hedges. These useful plants are not hard to grow; give them a well-drained position in a fertile soil. Add organic matter to the ground when planting to give them a good start. They

Osmanthus x burkwoodii

will in time make quite large bushes up to around 3m (10ft) tall and the same across.

Osmanthus are useful for planting in front of other shrubs which may have become leggy at the base as they are well-furnished with foliage to ground level and can be easily prevented from growing too high. Propagate these plants from seed.

soil	Not fussy, as long as well drained and organic matter is added at planting time
watering	Keep plants well watered until established, when they should withstand dry spells
pruning/ thinning	None, unless growing these plants as clipped or shaped specimens. In that case, trim plants after flowering
general care	Easy to maintain and cultivate. An annual application of manure will improve growth
pests & diseases	Pests and diseases do not usually cause any problems. Osmanthus is relatively trouble free

	SPRING	SUMMER	AUTUMN	WINTER	height (cm)	spread (cm)	flower/leaf colour	
Osmanthus x burkwoodii	flowering, in leaf	in leaf	in leaf	in leaf	300	300	▨	Easy to grow evergreen; flowers are scented
O. delavayi	flowering, in leaf	in leaf	in leaf	in leaf, flowering	350	350	▢	Slightly earlier flowering; better fragrance

 flowering   in leaf

Pachysandra terminalis

This is a highly useful plant! It is a low, gound covering evergreen plant from north China and Japan that forms thick carpets of virtually weed proof growth, spreading steadily by underground stems. It is related to the common box and has foliage of a similarly glossy quality, although the leaves of Pachysandra are larger and have toothed margins.

In early summer, tufts of white flowers appear from the ends of the short stems, although plants are usually grown for their foliage. This is a very easy, hardy plant to grow and ideal for a shaded position. It is best to plant several small plants initially, in enriched, moist soil, but once plants are well established they will tolerate some dryness at the root without suffering. It is not fond of very chalky soil but will grow fairly well in alkaline ground as long as it is moist.

Allow Pachysandra to spread freely under larger shrubs to cover bare soil. In woodland situations, it can be planted to form rivers of green that can be kept neat by careful trimming. It is also at home in oriental themed parts of the garden. Pachysandra even works well as a covering to specimens planted in large containers.

There is a variegated selection that has foliage splashed with white, but the leaves are rather deformed-looking and the white of the leaves has a rather dirty look to it. The plain green is usually superior.

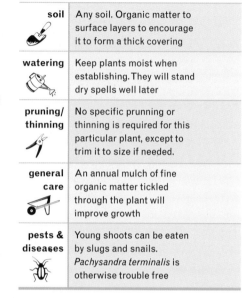

soil	Any soil. Organic matter to surface layers to encourage it to form a thick covering
watering	Keep plants moist when establishing. They will stand dry spells well later
pruning/ thinning	No specific prunning or thinning is required for this particular plant, except to trim it to size if needed.
general care	An annual mulch of fine organic matter tickled through the plant will improve growth
pests & diseases	Young shoots can be eaten by slugs and snails. *Pachysandra terminalis* is otherwise trouble free

Propagate plants by simply detaching rooted stems and placing them into pots of compost until the plantlets have properly established themselves.

Pachysandra terminalis

Plants for Shade

Philadelphus

Mock orange

These well-known plants are usually thought of as large, rather ungainly, suckering shrubs with strongly scented white flowers produced in early summer, but with few other virtues in the garden. However there are cultivars that are of great value in shaded sites. Perhaps most useful of all is *P. coronarius* 'Aureus'. This more compact growing plant has leaves of a wonderful golden-yellow in spring and early summer.

As summer progresses, the foliage tones down to light green. In shade this plant is seen at its best, as the foliage does not burn, which can be a problem in sunny areas; instead, the leaves are a more lime-green colour. Clusters of small, white flowers appear in early summer, but are not showy beside the foliage. It is useful planted with other darker-leaved plants to provide a splash of bright colour; it also combines well with lower growing spring bulbs and herbaceous plants such as hellebores and Pulmonaria.

If you are looking for highly scented flowers, try *P.* 'Belle Etoile' that produces many mauve-centred, white flowers in mid-summer. This plant will not bloom in the deep shadows, but positioned in light dappled shade it will perform well. The pale

Philadelphus 'Virginal'

soil	Not generally fussy; will grow in quite poor soils as long as not too soggy
watering	Keep plants moist when establishing. If they get too dry, foliage soon suffers
pruning/ thinning	Cut out old wood from inside the plant occasionally to encourage fresh new shoots
general care	It is very easy to grow these plants. Spread some manure around their roots occasionally
pests & diseases	Blackfly and powdery mildew can occasionally be troublesome to Philadelphus

Philadelphus 'Belle Etoile'

flowers show up well in such positions, and the fragrance produced by them is particularly charming in the early evening.

Generally, these plants will grow in most fertile soils, provided they do not get too wet. They must be kept moist while establishing, but after a few years plants will tolerate dry periods well. Propagate Philadelphus from softwood cuttings taken in summer.

	SPRING			SUMMER			AUTUMN			WINTER			height (cm)	spread (cm)	flower/leaf colour	
Philadelphus 'Belle Etoile'		in leaf	in leaf	flowering	in leaf	in leaf	in leaf	in leaf					250	230		For light shade, plants will fail to bloom. Powerful fragrance
P. coronarius 'Aureus'		in leaf	flowering	flowering	in leaf	in leaf	in leaf	in leaf					150	130		Wonderful plant for brightening a gloomy corner
P. 'Virginal'		in leaf	in leaf	flowering	flowering	in leaf	in leaf	in leaf					300	250		Very fragrant, pure white flowers

flowering · in leaf

P

Plants for Shade

Phyllostachys

This genus of bamboos contains some of the best of all for general use in the garden and most are not too invasive, spreading by runners that are easily controlled. These fine evergreen plants help to lend an oriental or exotic appearance to the garden, and the sound of the breeze passing through an established clump is wonderful.

Over a few years a substantial clump will be formed; some species of Phyllostachys also grow to a considerable height, over 4–5m (13–16ft) is quite possible in good conditions. Many Phyllostachys are grown for their attractively coloured stems (culms). *Phyllostachys nigra* has culms that are near black, *P. aurea*'s are golden green while those of *P. bambusoides* 'Castilloni' are yellow with green stripes. The qualities of the stems are best observed if the lower branches are removed. This also allows the light to pass through, giving the clump a lighter, more graceful appearance. Removing a few of the oldest culms (which are usually the thinnest from within the clump) every year also helps to enhance this characteristic and will provide a supply of sturdy canes to use in the garden.

Plant these bamboos in a fertile, moist, but well-drained position and add plenty of organic matter at planting time. Keep moist until established. Every spring, as new shoots emerge, clear away old leaves from inside the clump before applying a thick mulch of manure. These bamboos are good candidates for growing in large containers so long as they are kept moist. Propagate through division of clumps in late summer, cut culms down by about half and replant in improved soil.

Phyllostachys aurea

Phyllostachys nigra

soil	Like a moist, well drained soil with plenty of organic matter. Not fussy over pH
watering	Keep plants well watered especially when establishing or in dry periods
pruning/ thinning	Remove old canes from inside the clump to allow light through. Cut off lower branches to show off culms
general care	Easy to maintain, apply a thick mulch of well rotted manure around clumps every spring
pests & diseases	Generally trouble free as there are not usually any problems with pests and diseases

Phyllostachys bambosoides 'Castilloni'

	SPRING	SUMMER	AUTUMN	WINTER	height (cm)	spread (cm)	culm colour	
Phyllostachys aurea	🌿🌿🌿	🌿🌿🌿	🌿🌿🌿	🌿🌿🌿	4-600	400+		Easy and quick to bulk up, makes a good hedge
P. bambosoides 'Castilloni'	🌿🌿🌿	🌿🌿🌿	🌿🌿🌿	🌿🌿🌿	7-900	700+		Better stem colour in light shade
P. nigra	🌿🌿🌿	🌿🌿🌿	🌿🌿🌿	🌿🌿🌿	4-600	400+		Wonderful stems, which turn black in the second year
P. viridiglauscens	🌿🌿🌿	🌿🌿🌿	🌿🌿🌿	🌿🌿🌿	900	700+		Huge, elegant plant for the larger garden

🌿 in leaf

Pieris
Forest flame

These popular evergreen shrubs are easily overlooked in the summer but are a spectacular sight in spring, producing displays of flowers and often vibrantly coloured young leaves. The long drooping racemes of usually white, bell-shaped blooms appear first, and are follwed by the young shoots that may be red or pink-tinted.

However, these shoots are usually produced before the risk of frost has passed and are easily scorched if temperatures fall too low. Some selections have flowers that are pink tinted, or young leaves that are bronzy. There are also variegated forms that are good for bringing a touch of brightness in summer to mixed plantings of spring flowering shrubs. Indeed, Pieris are often grown with other acid-loving species such as rhododendrons, but it is best to try to position them with plants which will provide some interest in late summer, such as Stuartias and Eucryphias. For drama, try growing the scarlet flowered climber *Tropaeolum speciosum* over well-established plants. After many years plants can become quite large and almost tree-like.

Pieris are a genus of plants that demand to be grown in acidic soil, but they will do well in containers of ericaceous compost for those who garden in a limey soil. When planting, choose a spot with moist soil, and include plenty of leaf mould to get plants off to a good start. Remove any seedpods that develop after the flowers have faded as

Pieris 'Forest Flame'

soil	Acidic, well-drained soil essential. Add organic matter when planting
watering	These plants like to be moist and soon suffer if they dry out
pruning/ thinning	No pruning is usually required for this plant. However, if required, it can be pruned to restrict spread
general care	For this plant, only an annual mulch of well rotted manure is much appreciated
pests & diseases	Phytophthora root rot can be a problem, but Pieris is otherwise trouble free from pests and diseases

these spoil the plant's appearance. Propagation is rather tricky; try taking soft tip or semi-ripe cuttings in summer.

Pieris japonica 'Debutante'

	SPRING	SUMMER	AUTUMN	WINTER	height (cm)	spread (cm)	flower/leaf colour	
Pieris 'Forest Flame'	● ● ●				300	200		Wonderful, invaluable plant; new foliage red
P. japonica 'Debutante'	● ●				130	100		Ideal for a container; new foliage coppery
P. japonica 'Pink Delight'	● ●				230	200		Grown for its showy, pink-tinged flowers

 flowering   *in leaf*

Polygonatum
Solomon's seal

These herbaceous plants are a common sight in cottage gardens, where they are valued for their elegant and rather unusual appearance. Spreading freely by fleshy rhizomes that lie just under the soil, in spring they send up tall shoots clad with oval soft grey-green leaves. The shoots then gently arch over to the horizontal about half way along their length.

In late spring, small bell-shaped white and green flowers dangle daintily from them. These plants are ideal for a soil that is constantly cool and moist and repay the addition of extra humus into the ground by producing taller stems, so apply an annual mulch of manure around plants in the spring. Their running habit makes them ideal for threading among low growing plants such as hostas and ferns, the tall stems adding a touch of height.

These plants are particularly well suited to growing under trees, where they enjoy the cool humidity.

Polygonatum are not good candidates for growing in containers due to their need for a free root run. In summer plants can be severely checked by attack from sawfly larvae that appear as tiny grey-green caterpillars, munching away the leaves to ribbons. As they gradually get fatter these grubs are easily spotted and can be picked off plants. As the season progresses, small blue berries may appear, replacing the flowers, while in autumn the leaves turn a fine butter yellow before the shoots finally die off, at which stage they should be cut to the ground.

Propagate Solomon's seal by division in the spring.

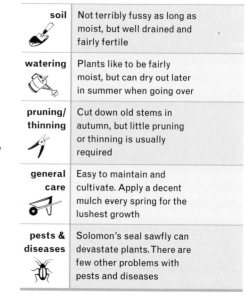

Polygonatum x hybridum

Polygonatum x hybridum

soil	Not terribly fussy as long as moist, but well drained and fairly fertile
watering	Plants like to be fairly moist, but can dry out later in summer when going over
pruning/ thinning	Cut down old stems in autumn, but little pruning or thinning is usually required
general care	Easy to maintain and cultivate. Apply a decent mulch every spring for the lushest growth
pests & diseases	Solomon's seal sawfly can devastate plants. There are few other problems with pests and diseases

	SPRING	SUMMER	AUTUMN	WINTER	height (cm)	spread (cm)	flower/leaf colour	
Polygonatum canaliculatum	🍃🍃	✹✹🍃	🍃🍃		150	60	▊	Largest growing Solomon's seal. A super garden plant
P. x hybridum	🍃🍃	✹✹🍃	🍃🍃		90	30	▊	Common and charming, great with ferns

 ✹ flowering   🍃 in leaf

P

Polypodium vulgare

Polypody

This versatile fern is one of the easiest of all to grow. It has long, narrow bright green evergreen fronds that are produced from a slowly creeping root, forming a mat of foliage about 30cm (12in) tall. It will make fine ground cover when established.

Plant polypody in a moist spot with some added organic matter, but after it has settled in it will tolerate quite dry conditions in even deep shade. It is a very easy plant to grow and needs little or no extra care,

soil	Not fussy regarding soil, but best in a well drained organic rich soil
watering	Keep plants well watered, withstands dry spells better than some ferns
pruning/ thinning	Very little pruning is ever required, although it can be prunned or thinned to restrict spread
general care	Easy to maintain. A little organic matter applied around the clump from time to time will help it grow
pests & diseases	Relatively trouble free. There are no problems in terms of pests and diseases

except an occasional tidy, removing any old or brown leaves. Plants will also respond well to a spring mulch of well rotted manure or leaf mould. In some areas, this fine plant grows epiphytically on tree branches, a habit which may be mimicked in the garden. If you have an old tree with a hole in the trunk or main branch, position a small piece of polypody in it and tie it in place, pressing in some lawn moss and a little compost to enable it to establish.

Alternatively, simply plant this fern conventionally in the ground, mixing it with other woodland plants. Its evergreen qualities can be useful in the garden, providing a good foil for plants such as spring-flowering bulbs and hellebores that bloom before much other foliage has emerged. It also makes a suitable plant for a winter pot or hanging basket. Propagation is easy; simply remove a piece of rooted rhizome and replant, removing some of the larger leaves and keeping the division well-watered until it begins to grow away.

Polypodium vulgare

P

Plants for Shade

Polystichum
Shield fern

These substantial, hardy, evergreen ferns are particularly easy to grow and some will even survive well in dry shade. There are several species often offered. *Polystichum aculeatum* is the hard shield fern, a particularly elegant fern with long, arching fronds that are a bright yellowish green in spring when just emerging.

As the season progresses, these leaves turn a rich glossy green, an attribute which is particularly useful during late autumn and winter. In good rich conditions the shuttlecocks of growth may reach 80cm (31in) tall.

Bigger still is a North American native, *P. munitum*, which is probably the best fully hardy evergreen fern of all. In good conditions the large clumps of glossy dark green foliage may reach 1m (3ft) in height and as much in spread, the crowns multiplying freely when happy. The evergreen fronds are wonderful in the winter and are excellent if used with winter flowering plants, showing off the other plants well. The most often seen of all is *P. setiferum*, the soft shield fern, of which there are many different selections with variously dissected and formed fronds. This is perhaps the toughest and most useful of its genus, thriving particularly well in dry shade. The foliage is delicate looking and

soil	Best in well drained, moist soil with plenty of humus. Some take dryer sites
watering	Keep plants moist to begin with. Will stand a surprising amount of drought
pruning/ thinning	Cut away tatty old fronds in spring as new ones unfurl. Little else is usually required
general care	This plant is generally easy to maintain and cultivate, apply a mulch every spring
pests & diseases	Is relatively trouble free. There are not usually any problems in terms of pests and diseases

remains most attractive until mid-winter, when hard frosts will start to damage foliage. More leaves are produced in spring, however, and are most attractive when unfurling.

Grow these plants with pale coloured flowers such as wood anemones and white-flowered Digitalis for a striking display. Plants will grow well in containers for a while. Propagate plants by division of clumps in spring.

Polystichum setiferum

	SPRING	SUMMER	AUTUMN	WINTER	height (cm)	spread (cm)	leaf colour	
Polystichum aculeatum	🍃🍃🍃	🍃🍃🍃	🍃🍃🍃	🍃🍃🍃	90	60		Attractive and elegant fern with glossy foliage
P. munitum	🍃🍃🍃	🍃🍃🍃	🍃🍃🍃	🍃🍃🍃	100	100		Spectacular large fern; fine in winter
P. setiferum	🍃🍃🍃	🍃🍃🍃	🍃🍃🍃	🍃🍃🍃	100	100		Tough and easy fern, even in dry shade

🍃 in leaf

Primula
Primrose

The common *Primula vulgaris* or primrose is one of the most charming and easily grown of all early spring flowers, with its little blooms of pale yellow or white, appearing just after the snowdrops have faded. It will grow well in some degree of shade, freely seeding around when happy, although it will not thrive in the very darkest corners of the garden.

There are many selected forms and hybrids with different coloured flowers, or even double blooms.

Plant common primroses in spring when they are most often available, in a moist position with some added organic matter to help retain moisture in summer.

Rather similar but generally smaller are the *P.* 'Wanda'

Primula vulgaris

soil	Moist and fertile. Some stand being waterlogged as long as not stagnant
watering	Moisture continually essential; *P. vulgaris* and *P.* 'Wanda' take drier conditions
pruning/ thinning	Cut away spent herbaceous growth at the end of the season. Little else is usually required
general care	Generally easy to maintain and cultivate. However, do mulch very regularly with manure
pests & diseases	Vine weevils and aphids may attack plants. No other problems with pests and diseases

cultivars, which generally have deeply coloured foliage and blooms in usually rich hues. These can make good perennials and tend to have a long flowering season over spring.

Very much larger is *P. florindae*, a plant for wet conditions in dappled shade. It forms a clump of large, rounded leaves from which tall flower spikes emerge in summer. Dangling yellow flowers that have a slight scent appear and continue in condition for several weeks. When plants are happy they will seed about. Give this plant plenty of manure, applied as a mulch in spring. *P. japonica* likes similar conditions and is one of several species known as 'candelabra primulas', having tall stems of flowers, the blooms arranged in whorls.

	SPRING	SUMMER	AUTUMN	WINTER	height (cm)	spread (cm)	flower colour	
Primula florindae					70	60		Magnificent species, the flowers held atop on tall stems
P. japonica					60	60		Needs constant moisture. One of easiest candelabra types
P. vulgaris					20	20		Easy and wonderful in early spring
P. 'Wanda'					10	20		Tiny but with masses of flowers

flowering

Pulmonaria
Lungwort

These plants are invaluable in the spring garden, providing long-lasting displays of floral colour, while forming fine ground cover later in the season, with dense mats of bristly, often attractively marked oval leaves. Pulmonarias come into flower in early spring, the small tubular blooms are produced in shades of purple, blue, pink, red or white before the large oval leaves begin to expand and cover the soil.

These plants are ideal under trees or at the front of the shaded border, so long as they do not get too hot or dry. These conditions will cause mildew to disfigure the foliage; if it strikes, simply chop off all the leaves, and feed and water well. Fresh new foliage quickly emerges.

Pulmonarias look wonderful with spring bulbs and hellebores, as they are usually lower growing and will quickly fill in any empty patches, and they continue to flower until early summer.

Pulmonaria rubra

Pulmonaria officinalis

soil	Soil should be kept very moist, but well drained and humus rich
watering	Try to keep plants fairly moist, or else foliage will quickly suffer
pruning/ thinning	Cut off any dried or mildewed leaves. Flower stems can also be removed if required
general care	An annual mulch is beneficial in spring. Little else is otherwise required to maintain this plant
pests & diseases	Powdery mildew can be a problem in dry conditions, and slugs and snails may also be a problem

Plant Pulmonarias in a well-drained position, with plenty of added organic matter. Once established, they will survive some drought but foliage will suffer, so it is better to keep plants moist if possible. These plants are not ideal for growing in pots, they usually become untidy quickly once they have flowered, far better to plant in the ground. Propagate from division of clumps after flowering.

	SPRING	SUMMER	AUTUMN	WINTER	height (cm)	spread (cm)	flower colour	
Pulmonaria angustifolia	● ●	◊ ◊ ◊ ◊ ◊			30	45		Fine elegant plant, slightly larger than many
P. 'Glacier'	● ●	◊ ◊ ◊ ◊ ◊			25	30		Subtle hint of blue in flowers is attractive
P. longifolium 'Bertram Anderson'	● ●	◊ ◊ ◊ ◊ ◊			35	45		Fine long, narrow spotted foliage, excellent flowers
P. 'Mournful Purple'	● ●	◊ ◊ ◊ ◊ ◊			20	30		Sombre flower colour; spotted leaves
P. officinalis	● ● ●	◊ ◊ ◊ ◊			25	45		Easy to grow, good ground cover; spotted leaves
P. rubra	● ●	◊ ◊ ◊ ◊ ◊			40	80		Large growing species; good flower colour
P. saccharata 'Leopard'	● ● ●	◊ ◊ ◊ ◊			30	50		Excellent spotted foliage and attractive blooms
P. saccharata 'Mrs Moon'	● ● ●	◊ ◊ ◊ ◊ ◊			30	50		Good, reliable, floriferous hybrid
P. saccharata 'Sissinghurst White'	● ● ●	◊ ◊ ◊ ◊ ◊			30	50		Lovely for its pure white flowers. Great with emerging ferns

● flowering ◊ in leaf

Rhododendron

Well known and much loved by gardeners, rhododendrons are some of the most spectacular of all flowering plants, and most prefer a position in some shade. They have one other essential requirement: they demand an ericaceous soil, which means that those who live in areas with an alkaline soil must grow them in large containers or raised beds filled with acidic compost.

Many really get too large for this treatment, which means cultivars must be chosen with care if they are to be kept in containers indefinitely. Look out for the yakushimanum hybrids, that tend to be compact and well suited to pot life.

Rhododendrons are generally thought of as being spring flowering plants, but some bloom earlier, even during winter, while others will flower well into summer, such as superb *Rhododendron* 'Polar Bear' which has trusses of large, scented, white flowers in July. The early-flowered types are often damaged by spring frosts in cold areas. Many are evergreen, but there are some that lose their leaves. The flowers come in a vast range of colours, almost every hue is

Rhododendron 'Morning Cloud'

represented, and some also have a powerful fragrance. Their biggest drawback is that after blooming, they take up a lot of space and have few other virtues, although some do have handsome foliage. Few plants will grow under large, well-established rhododendrons, so it is important to include other plants that will prolong the season of interest, either with later flowers or attractive leaves. Helpfully there are some cultivars that have variegated foliage

Rhododendron 'Golden Torch'

Rhododendron 'Sapphire'

soil	For rhododendrons, soil should be acidic, free-draining and humus rich
watering	Keep well watered once establishing, plants will not tolerate much drying out
pruning/ thinning	None is really required. However slight pruning or thinning can be administrated
general care	Easy once established, old flowerheads can be removed where possible, and an annual spring mulch
pests & diseases	There are many problems with vine weevils, bud blast, leaf hoppers and Phytophthora root rot

Rhododendron 'Daviesii'

Rhododendron 'Addy Wery'

Rhododendron 'Pink Pearl'

making them of greater value in the smaller garden. When planting a rhododendron, choose a well-drained site that is constantly moist. Plants hate becoming too dry and will suffer in drought, the leaves curling and hanging limply. Add plenty of well-rotted manure, and do not plant too deeply; plants that are too deep will sit and sulk for years, producing no flowers and little new growth.

When the flowers have faded it is best to remove old flowerheads. Twist them off with care or you may end up pulling off the new shoots as well! Propagate plants by layering, or from semi ripe cuttings taken in summer.

	SPRING	SUMMER	AUTUMN	WINTER	height (cm)	spread (cm)	flower colour	
Rhododendron 'Addy Wery'					100	150		Glossy foliage and an abundance of flowers
R. 'Daviesii'					150	150		Has very fragrant flowers
R. 'Golden Torch'					150	150		Compact growing with wonderful flower colour
R. Knaphill Hybrids 'Persil'					200	200		Deciduous type with fragrance. Brightens up a dark spot
R. luteum					300	300		Wonderful fragrance; deciduous; only for light shade
R. 'Morning Cloud'					150	150		Compact growth, large leaves
R. 'Olive'					100	100		Wonderful for its early flowers. Compact, so fine for a pot
R. 'Pink Pearl'					400	400		Large, easy hybrid
R. 'Percy Wiseman'					200	200		Compact and low growing; good for smaller gardens
R. 'Polar Bear'					400	400		Scented and spectacular late flowers. Large plant
R. ponticum 'Variegatum'					500	500		Large, but with most attractive foliage for year round interest
R. 'Sapphire'					100	100		Compact habit, small, glossy leaves
R. yakushimanum					200	200		Compact and good for a pot, many fine hybrids. Good leaves

flowering ⊘ in leaf

Ribes
Flowering currant

With dangling racemes of dainty reddish-pink flowers held against fresh green leaves in the spring, the popular shrub flowering currant, *Ribes sanguineum*, is a good choice for an early-flowering plant, as it is tough and easy to grow. It is also tolerant of a wide range of conditions, although not suited for deep shade.

There is also a charming white-flowered selection, *R. sanguineum* 'White Icicle' which shows up particularly well in dappled shade. Look out for the golden leaved selection, *R. sanguineum* 'Brocklebankii', which is of great value in shade.

Some people are not keen on the pungent odour given off by these plants, so they may be best planted towards the back of the border, where they can spread out well. In summer these plants are not of high value and make good subjects for growing a flowering climber up. Less commonly seen is *R. speciosum*, a species that is well

Ribes sanguineum 'Pulborough Scarlett'

soil	Not fussy; will grow well in clay as long as not waterlogged
watering	Keep establishing plants well moist, but do not waterlog them
pruning/thinning	Plants can be trimmed after flowering if required, but little else is usually needed for this plant
general care	Generally easy to maintain and cultivate, and an occasional mulch will encourage good growth
pests & diseases	Aphids and powdery mildew can attack plants, but generally pests and diseases are not a problem

suited for growing on cool shaded walls. It has stems covered in spines and small shiny leaves. In early spring, dangling flowers appear of a rich red that resemble tiny fuchsia blossoms. Trained on a pale coloured wall it creates an arresting sight.

R. laurifolium also flowers early. This is a neat, desirable evergreen shrub that produces dangling bunches of pale green flowers. The leaves are dark and oval and serve as a good foil for the blooms, which are easily damaged by frost. Plant Ribes in a well-drained situation with added organic matter, although they are not particularly fussy over soil.

	SPRING	SUMMER	AUTUMN	WINTER	height (cm)	spread (cm)	flower colour	
Ribes laurifolium	● ● 🌿🌿	🌿🌿🌿	🌿🌿🌿	🌿🌿🌿	100	100		Good for its early flowers and evergreen habit
R. sanguineum 'Brocklebankii'	● ● 🌿	🌿🌿🌿			120	120		Excellent for enlivening shade with its golden leaves
R. sanguineum 'King Edward VII'	● ● 🌿	🌿🌿🌿			250	250		Typical flowering currant, light shade only
R. sanguineum 'Pulborough Scarlett'	● ● 🌿🌿	🌿🌿			250	250		Similar to above
R. sanguineum 'White Icicle'	● ● 🌿🌿	🌿🌿			200	200		Makes an attractive change from the red cultivars
R. speciosum	● ● 🌿🌿	🌿🌿🌿			200	200		Wonderful as a wall trained specimen

● flowering   🌿 in leaf

Rodgersia

If you are lucky enough to have a streamside garden, a bog garden or an area that is constantly moist, these wonderful, large-leaved perennials may be for you. Rodgersias produce some of the largest and most attractive foliage of any hardy plant, and many species also have large spires of small but eye-catching flowers during the summer.

Plants spread around slowly from a creeping rhizome and eventually form large clumps.

Most often seen is *Rodgersia pinnata*, an elegant plant with textural leaves that are held in pairs and may be bronze tinted in some selections. The fluffy-looking flowers appear at the top spike about 1m (3ft) high and are usually pale pink, but may be white or reddish-pink.

Magnificent *R. aesculifolia* has foliage rather similar in appearance to that of the horse chestnut tree, but is usually bronze-tinted and hairy. It is a large species, white flower stems holding whitish flowers may reach almost 2m (6ft) in good conditions. Just as large, and arguably the most desirable, is *R. podophylla*, with huge leaves divided into five leaflets with serrated edges. This is bronze tinted when young. The flowers are white. In autumn, the foliage of this species turns bright red and is most spectacular.

soil	Soil should be kept constantly moist, and humus rich
watering	Never let plants get too dry, or the foliage will suffer. Try to keep them fairly moist
pruning/ thinning	No specific pruning is required. However, cut off dead foliage at the end of the season
general care	Simply apply a thick mulch of well rotted manure every spring. Little else is required
pests & diseases	Slugs and snails can damage emerging leaves, however pests and diseases are not usually a problem

Plant all species in spring, improving the site well with organic matter. They must have a rich, cool, constantly moist soil. They will not thrive in deep shadows but revel in semi and dappled shade. Grow with hostas, ferns and other moisture lovers. Propagate plants from division on rhizomes in spring. These plants are not suited to growing in containers.

Rodgersia aesculifolia

	SPRING	SUMMER	AUTUMN	WINTER	height (cm)	spread (cm)	flower colour	
Rodgersia aesculifolia	in leaf	flowering/in leaf	in leaf		200	100		Huge plant in the correct spot, great textured foliage
R. pinnata 'Superba'	in leaf	flowering/in leaf	in leaf		100	80		The most often seen and the best for a small garden
R. podophylla	in leaf	flowering/in leaf	in leaf		150	150		Excellent autumn tints, great leaf shape

● flowering   🗡 in leaf

Plants for Shade

Roscoea

These charming little plants are members of the ginger family and have recently become more popular in gardens, their exotic foliage and flowers bringing a touch of the tropics to temperate climes, although for a decent range you will need to visit a specialist nursery.

Some of these plants are fairly hardy and will stand a good deal of frost, provided they are planted in a well drained spot and covered with a thick over wintering mulch of organic matter. Roscoeas are herbaceous and emerge in late spring from fleshy roots that should be planted deeply during the summer. Do watch for late frosts that may damage growth as it emerges; cover plants with horticultural fleece to protect them.

Roscoeas are not too fussy over soil type, and will grow in limey ground as long as it does not get too dry. They are not for deep shade, but do well in woodland conditions where they are of considerable value, flowering later than many other plants usually grown here. They are also ideal for a shaded rock garden.

Roscoea cautleoides is a charming little plant, with narrow, upright foliage and small clusters of usually pale yellow hooded flowers produced in late summer. Some

soil	Moist, cool, well drained and with added organic matter
watering	Do not let plants dry out. Keep them well watered and moist
pruning/ thinning	Simply remove any old, dead growth at the end of the season. Little else is required with this plant
general care	Generally easy to maintain and cultivate; however, an annual mulch will keep plants happy
pests & diseases	Slugs, snails and vine weevils are the only problems in terms of pests and diseases

selections of this species may have white or mauve flowers.

The other species becoming more common is the *R. purpurea*, with similar rich green foliage and attractive blooms of usually purple, mauve or even white.

These plants do not like too much competition and should be given a spot where they can grow freely, such as at the front of a border. Plants may be split carefully in spring.

Roscoea cautleoides

Roscoea cautleoides

	SPRING	SUMMER	AUTUMN	WINTER	height (cm)	spread (cm)	flower colour	
Roscoea cautleoides		✐ ✐ ✐ ● ● ✐			40	13		Late flowering. Good for shade, remember where planted
R. purpurea		✐ ● ● ● ● ✐			30	13		As above

 flowering   in leaf

Sambucus
Elder

A familiar British native, elder is an attractive plant found in hedgerows and other wild places, but there are some altogether more spectacular garden cultivars with gold and variegated foliage that are great for brightening semi-shaded areas of the garden.

They are easy to grow and undemanding over soil requirements as long as the ground is not waterlogged or bone dry. Elders are best planted in the autumn and given a hard prune in spring to encourage the production of the most attractive, brightly coloured young foliage. Include plenty of well-rotted manure when planting, to give plants a good start. As they are grown for their foliage, elders are best treated as a coppice, the shoots cut back annually to a low level. Grow these plants at the back of borders as

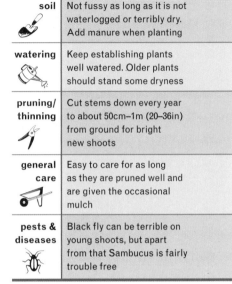

soil	Not fussy as long as it is not waterlogged or terribly dry. Add manure when planting
watering	Keep establishing plants well watered. Older plants should stand some dryness
pruning/ thinning	Cut stems down every year to about 50cm–1m (20–36in) from ground for bright new shoots
general care	Easy to care for as long as they are pruned well and are given the occasional mulch
pests & diseases	Black fly can be terrible on young shoots, but apart from that Sambucus is fairly trouble free

Sambucus nigra 'Black Beauty'

Sambucus racemosa 'Sutherland Gold'

a foil to plants in front, or use them to grow climbers through.

S. nigra 'Aurea' has foliage of gold, or more of a lime green in shade; in late summer, heads of white flowers may be produced. Similar, but with a finer, more fern-like leaf, is *S. racemosa* 'Plumosa Aurea'; in shade the normally golden leaves are a bright green. *S. nigra* 'Madonna' is attractive with green leaves edged with gold. There are selections with purple leaves of less value in shade, they simply disappear in to the shadows. Due to their quick growing habit these plants will fail in containers; they require plenty of room for their root systems. Propagate from softwood cuttings in summer or hardwood cuttings in winter.

	SPRING	SUMMER	AUTUMN	WINTER	height (cm)	spread (cm)	flower/leaf colour	
Sambucus nigra 'Aurea'	🍃	☀️🍃🍃	🍃🍃		400	400		Fine plant for shade; the golden leaves show up well
S. nigra 'Black Beauty'	🍃	☀️🍃🍃	🍃🍃		400	400		Glossy black foliage, pink scented flowers
S. nigra 'Madonna'	🍃	☀️🍃🍃	🍃🍃		200	200		Interesting alternative to the above. Less often seen
S. racemosa 'Plumosa Aurea'	☀️🍃🍃	🍃🍃	🍃		300	300		Wonderful dissected foliage; great in light shade
S. racemosa 'Sutherland Gold'	☀️🍃	🍃🍃	🍃		300	300		Very similiar to 'Plumosa Aurea'

☀️ *flowering*   🍃 *in leaf*

Sarcococca
Christmas box

Neat, easy to grow and evergreen, these low growing shrubs are a fine choice for a shaded spot, making tidy, mound-shaped bushes, covered in shiny, usually oval, dark green leaves. Plants spread by underground shoots, eventually forming quite large clumps. However, they play their trump card in winter.

Around mid-winter time, little white tassels appear, hidden under the leaves. These flowers may not be spectatular to look at, but they release a delicious, spicy perfume that is surprisingly pervasive. This asset makes it a good plant to put close to the house, where people will appreciate the fragrance. Alternatively, pieces may be cut and bought indoors, as branches last quite well in water. The flowers are followed by quite attractive glossy black or sometimes red berries which last on the plant right through the summer.

These plants are quite tolerant of a range of conditions; they will grow quite well on chalky soil and will take quite dry positions once established, but it pays to treat them well from the start, adding plenty of organic matter when planting. Avoid anywhere that is water logged. Planted en masse they will form good ground cover, but are at home under other larger shrubs or in a woodland position.

Plants will grow fairly well in containers for a while; this way they can be moved close to the house when in flower.

These plants are most easily propagated through division of established clumps, which is best done in spring. Divisions will sulk for a while before settling in to their new position. Mulch plants well in spring for the healthiest clumps.

soil	Not fussy, but best in a humus rich spot. Likes good drainage
watering	Keep plants moist; established specimens will take some dryness
pruning/ thinning	Pruning is not essential for Sarcococca, but it can be pruned to contain its growth
general care	Mulch with well-rotted manure every spring. Little attention is otherwise required to maintain growth
pests & diseases	Relatively trouble free. Does not have any particular problems with pests and diseases

Sarcoccoca confusa

	SPRING	SUMMER	AUTUMN	WINTER	height (cm)	spread (cm)	flower/leaf colour	
Sarcoccoca confusa					130	100		Easy, and has wonderful fragrance in the winter
S. hookeriana var. *digyna*					130	200		Most attractive long, pointed foliage

☀ *flowering*   🍃 *in leaf*

Sasa

These are some of the toughest of all bamboos, and have some of the most luxuriant foliage of any that are hardy. However, these virtues come with a distinct warning; they are very invasive and once established prove to be hard to get rid of.

The underground runners spread for long distances and will pop up unwanted in beds, borders and lawns, soon forming tall leafy shoots. *Sasa palmata* f. *nebulosa* will form a thicket up to 3m (10ft) high. The leaves are broad and oblong in shape, up to 30cm (12in) long, and held on narrow canes. It makes a fine hedge as long as the ground either side can be regularly mown, or even better, a trench, filled with concrete, can restrain the plant. Even then runners will hop over the top.

This plant will grow in a large container as long as it can be fed and watered enough.

soil	Tolerates any type of soil, so long as it is not too wet
watering	Plants like to be moist until established, then they will take long dry spells well
pruning/ thinning	Remove any old tatty stems in spring, but apart from that no special pruning required
general care	Easy to care for. Applying an annual mulch of manure in spring will keep growth healthy
pests & diseases	Relatively trouble free. Does not have any particular problems with pests and diseases

Sasa palmata f. nebulosa

Sasa palmata f. nebulosa

Similar but smaller is *S. veitchii*. This plant is about half the size of *S. palmata* f. *nebulosa* and rather less invasive, although still not suited for a small garden. It has margins that become bleached, giving a two-tone effect, which is rather striking from a distance, although the plant appears wind burned at close quarters.

If you have a suitable site for these plants, it is worth planting them well, for good establishment. They are tolerant of many sites, will survive some dryness at the root and will grow in quite deep shade, but they must not be waterlogged. Propagate plants from rooted runners.

	SPRING	SUMMER	AUTUMN	WINTER	height (cm)	spread (cm)	leaf colour	
Sasa palmata f. *nebulosa*	🍃🍃🍃	🍃🍃🍃	🍃🍃🍃	🍃🍃🍃	1000			Tough and will grow like mad, so not for small gardens
S. veitchii	🍃🍃🍃	🍃🍃🍃	🍃🍃🍃	🍃🍃🍃	800+			Effective foliage from a distance, less good close up

🍃 *in leaf*

Saxifraga
Saxifrage

There are few saxifrages that will thrive in the shaded garden; the more well-known alpine ones are plants for the sunny rockery. However there are species that are becoming more widely grown, which are most useful at the front of shady borders. *Saxifraga fortunei* is a leafy plant rather similar in appearance to a Heuchera, but the foliage has a more glossy, succulent appearance.

These plants are also fully herbaceous, dying down completely in the winter, to re-emerge in spring. The plant forms attractive rosettes of green, rounded leaves with reddish undersides. However, it is in late autumn that this plant is at its most valuable. Given a sheltered spot away from early frosts, airy spires of dainty star-shaped white blooms are produced that last for several weeks. Once these have faded the plant is usually caught by frost, which turns the fleshy foliage to mush. In recent years several selections of these plants have become available with coloured foliage, some tinted with bronze or red, or even splashed with pink. *S. fortunei* 'Black Ruby' is a particular favourite, with almost black foliage and pink flowers.

S. stolonifera or 'mother of thousands' is well known as a house plant, but will grow outside in many places, forming attractive ground cover with evergreen, oval leaves spreading freely via stolons.

Plant in a moist but well drained soil in semi-shade. Add plenty of fine organic matter to the soil and mulch lightly every year, if possible with leaf mould. They do not like too much competition, so grow them with plants of a similar size and do not let them to become encroached by over enthusiastic bedfellows. Propagate from division of established clumps; or from rooted stolons in the case of *S. stolonifera*, which is effective grown in a container where it spills over the edge.

Saxifraga stolonifera

soil	Soil should be kept moist but well drained, full of humus and rich
watering	Keep these plants watered regularly. Do not let them dry out
pruning/ thinning	No specific requirement, but saxifrages can be hard pruned as required to restrict spread
general care	Provide an annual mulch in spring, but apart from that, Saxifraga is generally easy to maintain
pests & diseases	Slugs and snails may munch foliage. Other than that, this plant is relatively trouble free

Saxifraga x urbium 'Variegata'

	SPRING	SUMMER	AUTUMN	WINTER	height (cm)	spread (cm)	flower/leaf colour	
Saxifraga fortunei					20	30		Excellent autumn flowering plant for a sheltered spot
S. fortunei 'Black Ruby'					20	20		Astonishing dark foliage
S. fortunei 'Cheap Confections'					20	20		Easy to grow. Flowers large and on short stems
S. fortunei 'Mount Nachi					20	20		Good foliage again
S. fortunei 'Rubrifolia'					20	20		Lovely foliage and flowers
S. stolonifera					20	30		Excellent gound cover for a sheltered spot. Earlier flowers
S. x urbium 'Variegata'					20	30		Excellent gound cover. Can withstand even deep shade

 flowering   in leaf

Schizophragma

If you are looking for a choice climbing plant that requires no trellis, clinging easily to walls and trees by itself in shade, Schizophragma may be the plant for you. However, you will need some patience to get the best from it.

They are similar to, and often confused with, the climbing hydrangea, *Hydrangea petiolaris*, but these deciduous plants are less often seen and in fact have more to offer the gardener, although they may require more care and attention, at least while establishing. Most often seen is *Schizophragma integrifolium*. This fine

Schizophragma hydrangeoides 'Moonlight'

soil	Like a well drained but moist, fertile soil. Plant close to support
watering	Keep plants moist when establishing, can be drier when well grown
pruning/ thinning	None usually required, if plants get too large, trim in spring to keep within bounds
general care	Quite easy when established. Tie in young plants carefully and mulch every year
pests & diseases	Relatively trouble free. Does not have any particular problems with pests and diseases

plant will take a while to get going, but in time produces oval, toothed, dark green leaves that set off the large heads of white flowers, each flower having a single large, showy bract when they appear in summer. The flowerheads last for many weeks, even into autumn.

S. hydrangeoides is similar, with long-lasting creamy heads of flowers and butter yellow autumn leaves. Even more desirable are selections from this plant.

S. hydrangeoides 'Roseum' has wonderful heads of pink flowers and is a fabulous sight in the garden. Grown for its foliage, *S. hydrangeoides* 'Moonlight' has leaves marbled with silvery grey, forming an unusual effect when covering a wall or up a tree.

These plants require a moist, organic rich soil that is well drained, so improve the soil when planting. If you wish to grow the plant up a wall, ensure that the climbing stems of the plant are in contact with it; even try using waterproof tape to attach it, although wire may be successful.

These plants are particularly fine grown up an old tree trunk. They like a cool shaded spot, but will not do well in the deepest shade. They will not thrive in a container. Propagate from semi-ripe cuttings in summer.

	SPRING	SUMMER	AUTUMN	WINTER	height (cm)	spread (cm)	flower/leaf colour	
Schizophragma hydrangeoides					100+	100+		More attractive. Flowers for longer than similar hydrangeas
S. hydrangeoides 'Moonlight'					100+	100+		Wonderful foliage. Best in light shade; has rather dark leaves
S. hydrangeoides 'Roseum'					100+	100+		Highly desirable form. Unlike any other plant
S. integrifolium					100+	100+		Slightly larger flowerheads than S. hydrangeoides

flowering   in leaf

Plants for Shade

S

Skimmia

These popular evergreen shrubs are often seen in gardens; they are valuable for their usually compact habit, fine glossy foliage and heads of fragrant flowers that appear in late winter. These flowers are often followed by clusters of showy red berries, so long as both male and female plants are grown in close proximity to each other. However it is unusual to see a well-grown specimen.

Many have a pale, undernourished look, or suffer from leggy growth or even dead patches. The problem usually lies in poor positioning of the plant from the outset. Skimmias are actually usually best-positioned in shade to prevent the leaves burning or turning an unhealthy shade of pasty green. However, they will not do well in very deep shade, so find a spot in dappled shade that is never waterlogged. When planting, add plenty of organic matter to the ground, especially if the soil is fairly alkaline; these plants will grow in chalky soil as long as it is not impoverished or bone dry. Ensure plants are well firmed in the ground at planting. Skimmias like a cool, fairly sheltered position and dislike becoming too dry, even once established. It is also important to keep plants well fed, so add a good mulch of well-rotted manure every year.

There are many different cultivars and if you are hoping for berries, you will need

Skimmia x confusa 'Kew Green'

soil	Skimmias like a fertile, well drained spot. Add organic matter when planting
watering	Plants should be kept moist, even when established. Do not let them dry out
pruning/ thinning	No specific requirement. However, Skimmia can be hard pruned to restrict spread
general care	An annual mulch will help keep plants in good condition. Other than that, Skimmia is easy to maintain
pests & diseases	Fairly trouble free from pests and diseases, but plants often look sick if soil is too dry or poor.

Skimmia japonica 'Rubella'

plants of both sexes. Most popular is *Skimmia japonica* 'Rubella', a male plant with dark green leaves and red tinted flowers, especially attractive in bud. *S.* 'Bronze Knight' makes a less compact plant with bronze tints to the foliage and similar flowers; it is also male. Perhaps the easiest to keep looking good is *S.* x *confusa* 'Kew Green'.

	SPRING	SUMMER	AUTUMN	WINTER	height (cm)	spread (cm)	flower/leaf colour	
Skimmia x *confusa* 'Kew Green'					200	200		Easy to grow with rather elongated leaves
S. japonica 'Bronze Knight'					150	200		Particularly good form with dusky foliage
S. japonica 'Rubella'					100	200		Flowers wonderful in bud, and have a fine scent. Compact

● flowering   🌿 in leaf

Smyrnium perfoliatum

There are few really first class annual or biennial plants that thrive in shade, so it is important to include this delightful species. This wonderful hardy plant has the general appearance of a Euphorbia and is often confused as such, although closer inspection reveals the plant to be a biennial member of the cow parsley family, Apiaceae.

The foliage is a lovely fresh green, especially in early summer, and plants grow to around 80cm–1m (30in–3ft) in height when in flower. The plant produces heads of lime green flowers, which are fairly small, but the effect is made all the more showy by the upper leaves, which are an acid yellow. The flowering stems appear in late spring and early summer. The plant has an almost two-tone look and creates a startling effect, especially in woodland, where drifts of this plant have an illuminating presence. Try mixing it with Myosotis that flowers at a lower level, or mingle it around the feet of flowering rhododendrons for a few shocking colour contrasts. The bright, limey greens of this plant's foliage really do set off the pinks, reds and whites of many plants. The form adds to the unusual effects that can be created with it in a shady garden.

Smyrnium perfoliatum likes a well drained, but humus rich soil in semi shade and once happy will seed readily about.

Grow plants initially from seed sown in situ or in a seed bed in spring, and plant out into position in summer. They will bloom the following year and these plants should produce self-perpetuating offspring to provide a succession of plants every year. These are really not plants for containers, as they tend to look spindly on their own. It is far better to plant them out en masse and in combinations with other plants.

Smyrnium perfoliatum

soil	For *Smyrnium perfoliatum*, soil should be kept well drained and humus rich
watering	Keep plants fairly moist, even if established, as they do not like dry ground
pruning/ thinning	Pull up old dead plants once they have seeded. Seedlings may need some thinning
general care	Generally very easy to maintain and cultivate. *Smyrnium perfoliatum* tend to look after themselves.
pests & diseases	Is relatively trouble free. Does not have any problems with pests and diseases

Smyrnium perfoliatum

Stewartia
Stuartia

Late-flowering shrubs are always of the highest garden value, as there are few which manage to provide much impact by the end of summer. Stewartias are an exception, although they have particular requirements and will eventually form a large, tree-like plant. Stewartias are hardy, deciduous plants and quite shrubby when young.

In mid-summer they produce attractive white flowers, rather like small, single camellia flowers. The blooms are produced for many weeks, although not usually in great profusion, until early autumn. At this stage the leaves develop reddish and orange tints, before eventually falling. As plants age, they become more tree-like with a distinct trunk; these trunks have fine flaking bark which provides a talking point in winter. Plant them with rhododendrons and camellias and other plants of spring interest to lengthen displays, or else team them with hydrangeas and other late flowering plants for maximum impact.

To grow well, these plants need a moist, well drained acidic soil in a sheltered corner, or under taller trees, and are best planted young, although plants are generally not particularly quick growing. Although they are eventually rather tall, they do not form bulky plants, making a slender tree in the end. *Stewartia malacodendron* will make a large shrub up to 5m (16ft) high; *S. pseudocamellia* will grow to the size of a small tree.

They enjoy having a little sun reaching their canopies when mature, but need their roots in shade, so they are suited to

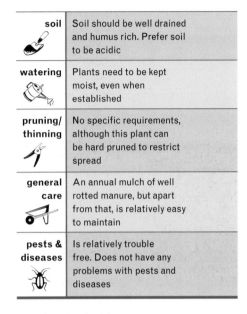

soil	Soil should be well drained and humus rich. Prefer soil to be acidic
watering	Plants need to be kept moist, even when established
pruning/ thinning	No specific requirements, although this plant can be hard pruned to restrict spread
general care	An annual mulch of well rotted manure, but apart from that, is relatively easy to maintain
pests & diseases	Is relatively trouble free. Does not have any problems with pests and diseases

dappled shade rather than deep shade, where they will eventually fail.

These plants will not do well if kept in containers for long; they eventually get too large, although it is possible to get them to flower in a large tub. Never let plants dry out.

Propagate plants from softwood cuttings in summer.

Stewartia pseudocamellia

Stewartia malacodendron

Symphytum
Comfrey

If you have a difficult dry, shaded area in the garden, you can almost be sure that Symphytum will manage to survive there. These lowish, ground-covering herbaceous perennial plants are able to grow in particularly poor situations, even by evergreen hedges, and are very easy to grow.

They are at their finest in spring, when they produce showy clusters of drooping flowers in a range of colours, although most are predominantly white. Their oval leaves are bristly and rather coarse but this foliage is thick and good at suppressing weeds when used as ground cover, perhaps under trees or on banks. Grow these plants to cover bare soil under large shrubs or in drifts under trees. They look good with Pulmonarias and hellebores. There are some particularly attractive variegated selections

soil	Not at all fussy. Will grow almost anywhere, even in dry shade
watering	Water plants until established. Only leaves will suffer in dry spells
pruning/ thinning	Cut back old flowering stalks and any other unwanted material. Can be pruned to restrict spread
general care	Generally easy to maintain and cultivate. Depending on conditions, they tend to look after themselves
pests & diseases	Relatively trouble free. Does not have any particular problems with pests and diseases

Symphytum

Symphytum

that need a little more light but make good foliage plants. They will grow in almost any soil and respond well to an annual mulch of manure in spring, tickled in between the stems. At this stage, plants are best tidied, and straggly pieces cut back and old tatty foliage removed. Plants can be rather vigorous and may need controlling if they are used around other slower-growing subjects. The leaves are excellent for composting or making a liquid feed.

Propagation could not be easier; simply detach a rooted stem and transplant. Comfrey is one of those useful plants you can always pull a piece off and fill a gap with. They are not ideal for containers are they are rather plain and unrefined up close.

	SPRING	SUMMER	AUTUMN	WINTER	height (cm)	spread (cm)	flower/leaf colour	
S. ibiricum (syn. grandiflorum)	● ●	● 𝄃 𝄃	𝄃 𝄃 𝄃		40	70		Good for poor soil in shade and most attractive in spring
S. orientale	● ● ●	● 𝄃 𝄃	𝄃 𝄃 𝄃		100	130		Easy and large growing, ideal for slightly rough locations

● flowering   𝄃 in leaf

Plants for Shade

S

Taxus
Yew

This tough, British native conifer is well known as a fine hedging plant, with its dark evergreen foliage and poisonous but attractive red berries. It is well suited for life in shade, and when established will tolerate dry conditions with ease. It can be clipped regularly, so is an ideal subject for topiary, rather like box.

Try clipping plants into large balls or cones and use these specimens to add a touch of formality to the shaded garden. As yew is by nature quite a dark plant, it makes a splendid foil for white or yellow flowers or plants with variegated foliage. *T. baccata* is lovely in spring; the new growth is a bright, fresh green. There are many different selections, some with golden foliage, others with a spreading habit making these

Taxus baccata 'Fastigiata Aurea'

soil	Not fussy, and can live in any soil, as long as it not too wet
watering	Keep establishing plants well watered. Survives periods of drought when older
pruning/ thinning	Trim hedges and topiary during the summer whenever it is required. Can also be pruned to restrict spread
general care	Generally easy to maintain and cultivate. Can be mulched with manure from time to time
pests & diseases	Relatively trouble free. Does not usually have any problems with pests and diseases

suitable as ground cover under trees or in problem areas. Pay a visit to a conifer nursery to choose the ones you like, most will be fine in shade. Particularly useful is *T. baccata* 'Fastigiata Aurea' which in time forms a narrow column of gold, and will add an impressive flash of light in the shadows.

Plant yew in a well drained soil, and improve the planting hole with well-rotted manure, as plants are likely to be in the same spot for many years; indeed they are among the longest lived of plants. Yew can be slow to establish and are never terribly rapid growing plants.

	SPRING	SUMMER	AUTUMN	WINTER	height (cm)	spread (cm)	leaf colour	
Taxus baccata	🍃🍃🍃	🍃🍃🍃	🍃🍃🍃	🍃🍃🍃	1500	800	▦	Tough and perhaps the best plant for hedging in shade
T. baccata 'Fastigiata Aurea'	🍃🍃🍃	🍃🍃🍃	🍃🍃🍃	🍃🍃🍃	600	300	▦	Excellent for introducing colour and interesting form to shade

🍃 *in leaf*

Tellima grandiflora

Fringe cups

Although never particularly showy, this charming woodland plant is a wonderful sight in flower; for the rest of the year the lobed evergreen foliage makes good ground cover. In spring, the fresh lime green leaves emerge and are swiftly followed by tall, airy spires of little green, bell shaped flowers that last for about a month.

This plant is best seen as a drift through woodland or in a border, or even under a tree. It needs to be mixed with other seasonal plants such as trilliums, ferns and *Milium effusum* 'Aureum' to be seen to best advantage. If you use them around shrubs, make sure there is enough height below the lowest branches for the tall flower spikes to develop and move in the breeze.

Tellima has a quality of astonishing freshness, almost capturing the essence of spring itself. After it has flowered, cut down flowering stalks as low as possible; resist the temptation to pull them off, you always end up uprooting whole sections of the plant. The leaves will overwinter, but may look shabby in spring; it is worth cutting off any which are in particularly bad shape before the new leaves appear from the top of the clump.

soil	Best in cool, moist well drained soil. Add organic matter when planting
watering	Keep plants moist when establishing. Will survive dry spells when established
pruning/ thinning	Cut down old flower stems by mid-summer, and remove any old, tatty leaves in the spring
general care	Generally easy to maintain and cultivate. Mulch in spring with manure for the best clumps
pests & diseases	Is relatively trouble free. Does not usually have any problems with pests and diseases

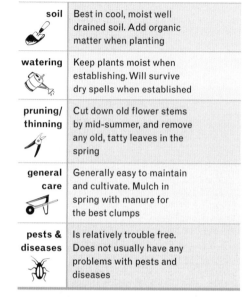

Tellima grandiflora

Tellima grandiflora

Tellima is easy to please. It will thrive in almost any soil, as long as it is moist but not wet. It will appreciate an annual mulch to really get it going well. The clumps will eventually become quite large, when they can be divided, usually after flowering. This serves as the perfect opportunity to get a good drift of clumps going. These are not good plants for containers.

Tiarella
Foam flower

These woodland plants of quiet charm and beauty are easily grown and will make good small-scale ground cover under and around larger plants. They are cultivated chiefly for their clumps of handsome foliage, rather like that of a diminutive heuchera. However, from late spring onwards, short spires of little, frothy pinkish-white flowers appear.

Tiarella wherryi is the species most often seen in cultivation and is compact and free flowering, but there are other slightly larger species, and recently some selections with coloured, marked or deeply indented foliage have become available. These are worth seeking out, as their form is interesting as well as their charming flowers.

Tiarella wherryi

Plant Tiarella in the spring. It will tolerate quite deep shade, but will only form good thick growth in moist, fertile soil, so add organic matter when planting.

Tiarella cordifolia

Plants spread from little runners that scramble over the soil surface, rooting as they go, forming new plantlets. This plant is not strictly an evergreen, although some foliage is often retained over winter. However, this quickly becomes rather untidy and should be cut away for the plant to look its best.

Fresh green foliage emerges in spring and is soon followed by the flowers. Tiarella looks good in drifts in a woodland planting, and also makes excellent edging to shaded beds and borders. It really is a useful plant, ideal for filling in small gaps or covering bare soil under shrubs.

This is not the sort of plant you would have as a specimen in a pot, but it could be used as part of a mixed planting, as the foamy flowers blend well with many other plants. Propagate from division of clumps in spring or from rooted runners.

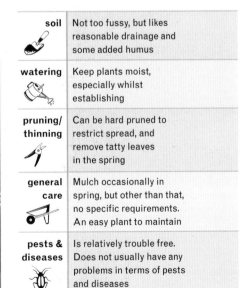
Tiarella wherryi

soil	Not too fussy, but likes reasonable drainage and some added humus
watering	Keep plants moist, especially whilst establishing
pruning/ thinning	Can be hard pruned to restrict spread, and remove tatty leaves in the spring
general care	Mulch occasionally in spring, but other than that, no specific requirements. An easy plant to maintain
pests & diseases	Is relatively trouble free. Does not usually have any problems in terms of pests and diseases

Trillium
Wake robin *or* Wood lily

This genus of choice woodland plants contains some of the most elegant of all plants that will grow in shade. These members of the lily family are easily recognized, as they always produce whorls of leaves and later petals in threes, produced atop a stout stem.

They appear from thick, fleshy roots, the shoots emerging rather like folded umbrellas. The green leaves when they expand may be blotched or splashed with mauve, and the flowers of white, pink, yellow or reddish mauve crown the shoot. Plants are at their wonderful best in mid-late spring. However Trilliums are not always easy to grow well, unless you can provide them with suitable conditions. They need a cool, moist well drained soil full of humus in a site where they will not get disturbed or overgrown by other more rampageous plants. Grow them with other choice woodland plants such as lilies and uvularias. Sometimes bare pieces of root are sold of certain species; these must be planted promptly, as old, dry pieces will usually fail. Plant them around 5cm (2in) deep. It is better to buy growing plants in pots and plant them in spring while flowering. Add leafmould at planting if possible and provide an annual mulch of it every spring. If you

Trillium grandiflorum

soil	Cool, organic rich, moist and well drained. Best plants usually on acid soil
watering	Moisture vital, especially in spring; less by late summer when becoming dormant
pruning/ thinning	Clear away faded stems in late summer, and can be hard-pruned to restrict spread
general care	An annual mulch of organic matter is about the only specific requirement. This results in the best clumps
pests & diseases	Slugs and snails may damage plants, but other than that it is relatively trouble free

cannot get leafmould, use some form of fine organic matter. Plants really need to be planted in the ground and given a free root run; they are no good in containers. Propagate plants by removing growing sections of root after plants have flowered.

Trillium grandiflorum

	SPRING	SUMMER	AUTUMN	WINTER	height (cm)	spread (cm)	flower/leaf colour	
Trillium erectum	flowering	in leaf	in leaf		30	30		Woodland plant, best seen en masse. Large species
T. grandiflorum	flowering	in leaf	in leaf		40	30		Most conventionally attractive and straight forward to grow
T. luteum	flowering	in leaf	in leaf		40	30		The flowers are sweetly scented, leaves mottled

☀ *flowering*   ⬋ *in leaf*

Plants for Shade

144

Tropaeolum speciosum
Flame flower

There are few climbing plants with flowers as brilliant a colour as those produced by the scrambling *Tropaeolum speciosum*. It is a perennial relative of the common nasturtium, but this species is a definite climber, and bears blooms of vibrant scarlet that form long-lasting garlands over shrubs and even hedging.

The plant emerges from the ground in the spring. Its stems are fleshy and rather brittle, but quick growing. It flowers from mid-summer until late in the growing season, often well into autumn, which makes it invaluable for bringing interest to plants that have bloomed earlier. Let it grow up rhododendrons, or better still scramble through yew hedges, where the dark green foliage acts as a perfect foil. The flame flower is really no good for growing up trellis, as it needs the more natural, informal support of other vegetation.

However, this plant is not always easy to establish, so do not expect rapid results. It does best in a cool, free draining, acidic rather sandy soil, although it needs some moisture during the growing season. It will not thrive in deep shade either, but light dappled conditions will suit it well. Try it on the north side of a hedge.

Tropaeolum speciosum

Plant *Tropaeolum speciosum* in spring in enriched soil and mulch the plant well with leafmould every year. It may take a further season to become properly established. Take care not to spear the rootstock out of the growing season.

This plant hates to be grown in a container and will not do well in such an environment. Propagate from division of established clumps, best done in early spring, or in autumn after flowering.

Tropaeolum speciosum

soil	*Tropaeolum speciosum* performs best in acidic, well drained and cool soil
watering	Plants like to be kept moist, especially whilst establishing, but not too wet
pruning/ thinning	No partivular pruning is needed apart from cutting away old growth at the end of the season
general care	Generally easy to maintain and cultivate. Simply mulch roots occasionally with leafmould
pests & diseases	Flea beetles and blackfly may attack plants. There are not usually problems with pests or diseases

Uvularia grandiflora

Merrybells

This charming woodland plant should be more widely grown. It is a herbaceous perennial, emerging each spring from the ground. The dainty, pale yellow, dangling, bell-shaped flowers have long twisted petals and hang from slender, rather arching stems that reach about 20–30 cm (9–12in) in height, and have narrow, oval greyish green leaves. The flowers open in mid-late spring and last for a couple of weeks.

The plant spreads slowly from a creeping rootstock. By late summer, the stems themselves begin to die down and may then be tidied away, simply snip off the stems at ground level. *Uvularia grandiflora* needs a well-drained but constantly moist cool soil with plenty of added organic matter, preferably leaf mould to grow and spread about. It looks particularly attractive grown towards the front of a shaded border. Mingle this lovely plant with small ferns, *Cyclamen hederifolium*, snowdrops (Galanthus) and other choice plants that appreciate similar conditions. It can look most attractive with *Brunnera macrophylla*, the clouds of blue flowers and heart shaped leaves providing a pleasing contrast, although ensure the brunnera does not encroach upon its more delicate planting partner.

Uvularia grandiflora will not thrive in containers as it needs a free root run and cooler soil conditions than can easily be achieved in a pot; besides, it is not in flower long enough to stand alone. Propagation is easy and is best carried out after flowering has finished. Simply divide established clumps, or detach a rooted piece of rhizome and plant it in improved soil and keep moist.

soil	Cool, moist, well drained. Alkaline soil if organic matter added regularly
watering	Keep plants moist; less so when dormant in late summer
pruning/ thinning	Cut any roots away once they have died, back in late summer. Otherwise little pruning is required
general care	Easy, simply apply a mulch in early spring of fine organic matter such as leafmould
pests & diseases	Slugs and snails can be a problem, but other than that, *Uvularia grandiflora* is relatively trouble free

Uvularia grandiflora

Vancouveria hexandra

Easy to grow and of a dainty nature, *Vancouveria hexandra* is a fine North American addition to the garden. It resembles a miniature Epimedium (a genus to which it is closely related) but has more rounded, almost hexagonal leaflets. The airy spires of little white and yellow flowers appear in spring, held above what is virtually evergreen foliage.

The whole effect is quietly attractive. When happy, the plant spreads quite quickly and will form large, rather open patches from its creeping rootstock. Eventually it makes good ground cover. Vancouveria like a cool, moist root run and will do best in woodland conditions with good drainage and plenty of added humus such as well-rotted manure. Plant it in semi shade rather than the darkest conditions and it should do well.

There are a couple of less often seen species of similar appearance that will thrive in the same conditions. It associates well with all manner of other plants; its diminutive stature makes it well sited for growing along the edges of borders. Alternatively, plant drifts of it under trees, mixing it perhaps with plants that have broader leaves such as *Asplenium scolopendrium*, hostas or bergenias to give a softer effect. Another good idea is to use it under shrubs to cover any unsightly bare ground.

This plant will grow for a while in a container; it is quite suitable for including as part of a mixed planting, or again for under planting a specimen shrub. Propagation is easy; simply divide clumps after flowering in late spring.

Vancouveria hexandra

soil	Cool, moist well drained. Add plenty of fine organic matter when planting
watering	Keep Vancouveria fairly moist, although ensure it is not too wet
pruning/ thinning	No pruning is really needed. However, to maintain shape, simply snip off any old untidy foliage
general care	Apply an annual mulch of leaf mould if possible in spring. Otherwise Vancouria is fairly easy to maintain
pests & diseases	Vancouveria is relatively trouble free. Pests and diseases do not usually create any problems

Plants for Shade

Viburnum

This large genus of popular, shrubby plants contains many which are of huge value to gardeners who have plots in shade. Most viburnums commonly encountered are straightforward to grow and relatively undemanding over soil type and subsequent aftercare. Some species are evergreen and provide valuable structure in the garden over winter, and others, while deciduous, are most attractive in spring when the fresh, bright green new growth appears.

Most viburnums produce showy heads of white flowers, usually between early spring and summer. These are often followed by attractive blue, red or even yellow berries.

Perhaps the best known is *Viburnum tinus* and its cultivars. These exceptionally easy to grow evergreen plants form large, dense

Viburnum tinus 'Gwenllian'

soil	Will grow in acid or alkaline. Add organic matter when planting. Avoid wet sites
watering	Water until established, should then tolerate some dryness
pruning/ thinning	If plant gets too large, it should be given a light trim. Remove any dead branches which may develop
general care	Is generally easy to maintain and cultivate, apply a mulch in spring for best growth
pests & diseases	Viburnum beetles can decimate plants in summer, causing foliage to reduce to tatters

bushes and will be in bloom for a tremendous length of time, right through the winter and on into summer, providing an invaluable long-term spread of colour in the shady garden. Some selections such as *V. tinus* 'Eve Price' are more compact growing, whereas others such as 'Gwenllian' have pink-tinted flowers. Particularly useful is the variegated selection that makes a bright, cheery, handsome foliage plant.

Also worth seeking out is the rather refined looking, purple tinged *V. tinus* 'Purpureum'. Small metallic blue berries often form on all these plants after flowering, sometimes while still in flower, adding to the display.

Majestic looking *Viburnum rhytidophyllum* is another evergreen, this time with large, elongated, downward pointing, slightly puckered leaves that have downy brown undersides. It is large growing but

Viburnum davidii

more open in habit than *V. tinus* and flowers in early summer.

Perhaps most desirable of all the viburnums is *V. davidii*, a terrifically useful plant in any garden that features a lot of shade. Low growing, compact and evergreen, it also has large, broad leaves and heads of white flowers in early summer, which are soon followed by showy metallic blue berries. More fruit will set if plants of both sexes are included in the garden.

Of the deciduous species, foremost must be *V. plicatum* 'Mariesii'. This wonderful plant needs plenty of space around it in order to look its best, but in the right conditions it will form a rounded, almost circular plant. It produces tiers of branches giving a layered effect that is accentuated when the heads of white flowers appear in early summer. The foliage is a fresh green and turns rich colours in autumn.

Viburnum opulus was a favourite during the 19th century that is still very popular today, forming ball like flowerheads of greenish white blooms in spring on a large shrub. It features attractive reddish berries that follow the blooms and its autumn colour is a reddish pink.

Viburnum tinus 'Eve Price'

	SPRING			SUMMER			AUTUMN			WINTER			height (cm)	spread (cm)	flower/leaf colour	
Viburnum davidii	🍃	🍃	●	●	🍃	🍃	🍃	🍃	🍃	🍃	🍃	🍃	100	100		Compact, neat and always of interest in the garden
V. opulus		🍃	●	●	🍃	🍃	🍃						300	300		Easy to please, but often affected by blackfly
V. plicatum 'Mariesii'		🍃	●	🍃	🍃	🍃	🍃						300	400		Fine flowers and good autumn tints. Needs space
V. rhytidophyllum	🍃	🍃	●	🍃	🍃	🍃	🍃	🍃	🍃	🍃	🍃	🍃	400	300		Elegant foliage plant for back of the border
V. tinus 'Eve Price'	●	●	●	●	🍃	🍃	🍃	🍃	🍃	●	●	●	200	200		Neat habit, pinkish flowers, good for small spaces
V. tinus 'Gwenllian'	●	●	●	●	🍃	🍃	🍃	🍃	🍃	●	●	●	300	300		Strong flower colour
V. tinus 'Purpureum'	●	●	●	●	🍃	🍃	🍃	🍃	🍃	●	●	●	400	500		Wonderful foliage effect, but a little dull in shade
V. tinus 'Variegatum'	●	●	●	●	🍃	🍃	🍃	🍃	🍃	●	●	●	300	300		Good bright foliage for shade

 flowering   in leaf

Vinca
Periwinkle

Tough, easy to grow and useful, Vinca is an essential plant for ground cover in shaded situations. The glossy, oval, evergreen leaves are held on soft arching stems or runners that spread out across the ground surface, rooting here and there as they go, and forming new plantlets.

In a short time, thick, weed-suppressing ground cover is provided, although in tidy gardens this plant is likely to quickly get out of control. Indeed the larger species, *Vinca major* is particularly rampageous and best suited to rough, slightly wild places. *V. minor* is a more delicate looking species, with smaller leaves and a neater, more creeping habit. It forms better-behaved ground cover under shrubs and other plants, although this too may need keeping in check. Simply cut away the growth that is not required to keep them tidy. This can be done at almost any time, but the end of the season may suit when the garden is being prepared for winter. At this stage any old dead stems are also best removed to improve the plants' appearance. Vinca are at their most attractive in late spring when the showy blue, white or purple five petalled flowers appear. Some selections have the added attraction of variegated foliage making them of even greater use in

Vinca minor 'La Grave'

soil	Almost any soil provided it is not waterlogged. Improve poor soils when planting
watering	Water well until established, when plants will take some drought
pruning/ thinning	To prune Vinca, cut off any runners which are taking over, and also remove any dead stems
general care	Give plants a tidy at the end of the year and apply the occasional mulch in spring. Otherwise, little needed
pests & diseases	Rust can prove to be a problem, but otherwise the plant has very few problems with pests and diseases

shade. These plants will grow in almost any soil and tolerate deep shade and some drought, especially when established. Some cultivars of *V. minor* make attractive plants to include in mixed containers, cascading down over the edges of the pot.

Vinca minor 'Gertrude Jekyll'

Vinca minor 'Atropurpurea'

	SPRING	SUMMER	AUTUMN	WINTER	height (cm)	spread (cm)	flower/leaf colour	
Vinca major					45	300+		Vigorous plant. Invasive tendencies
V. major 'Variegata'					45	300+		As above, but with colourful foliage ideal for shade
V. minor					15	300+		Better behaved and more suited to the smaller garden
V. minor 'Atropurpurea'					15	300+		Darker flower colour provides good contast to others
V. minor 'Gertrude Jekyll'					10	300+		Very compact. Dainty, slightly paler foliage than usual
V. minor 'La Grave'					15	300+		Fine cultivar

 flowering

Vitis coignetiae
Vine

There are few plants that can compare with this wonderful ornamental vine for the impact of their autumn foliage. It is a most vigorous plant when well established in suitable growing conditions, and is well able to climb to the tops of tall trees.

It has large, luxuriant, heart-shaped leaves that may be over 30cm (12in) long. These are deciduous and appear in the late spring from woody stems that have tendrils along them which the plant uses to climb. As autumn approaches, the leaves start to change from mid-green to a range of wonderful, fiery tones of rich red, scarlet and crimson, sometimes with splashes of orange. These leaves take around a month to fall and are best seen when the plant is allowed to clamber on to a dark-leaved evergreen such as a yew, or other trees with contrasting autumn leaf colour.

soil	Acid or alkaline and not waterlogged. Add organic matter when planting
watering	Keep *Vitis coignetiae* well watered until it is established
pruning/ thinning	Chop off any growth which threatens to overpower planting or smother trellis/pergolas
general care	Generally easy to maintain and cultivate. Can mulch around the roots with manure every spring
pests & diseases	*Vitis coignetiae* is relatively trouble free. Has no problems with pests and diseases

In smaller spaces the plant will be at home growing over a pergola or large trellis, although it will need to be kept in check.

This is not a plant for really dark spots, but it is able to scramble through the shadows up to find the sun, and will be happy in semi or dappled shade, especially lower down. When planting, find a good site for this vine, which is well drained yet fairly moist, and include plenty of organic matter to fuel it for vigorous, healthy growth.

It will not do well for long in even a large container, although it would probably look fine for two or three years. Propagate these plants from hardwood cuttings taken in late autumn.

Vitis coignetiae

V

Plants for Shade

Waldsteinia ternata

This semi-evergreen ground covering plant is in fact a member of the rose family. It creates an attractive, fairly loose carpet of soft green leaves that are divided into three leaflets. It produces pretty little yellow flowers during spring and early summer.

This plant spreads about in good conditions quite happily via runners, but it is easily controlled and rarely a nuisance. It is not a plant for the deep shadows, growing well only in dappled shade where plants will receive a little bright light. Neither is this plant fond of drying out, so ensure plenty of well-rotted organic matter is added to the area when you are planting. Waldsteinias' chief hate is waterlogged or heavy, soggy ground; plants will soon die out under these conditions so choose somewhere well drained. This plant grows well under and around shrubs, and looks particularly good tumbling down a bank where it will

Waldsteinia ternata

appreciate the free draining conditions. It is also attractive under trees and in a woodland setting, the soft slightly downy foliage contrasting with glossy leaves of hellebores, for example. In mild winters the plant may well retain some foliage, although it will be fairly untidy by spring. At this stage, snip back the old foliage and apply a good mulch of manure to encourage healthy shoots to emerge. This plant can be grown as an under planting to larger specimen plants in containers. Propagate by dividing clumps after flowering or by simply detaching rooted plantlets.

Waldsteinia ternata

soil	Free draining, moist and with plenty of added organic matter
watering	Keep plants moist, they will tolerate a little dryness once established
pruning/ thinning	Little pruning or thinning is needed, but can remove old and tatty leaves in the spring
general care	Generally easy to maintain and cultivate. Can apply a mulch of well rotted manure in spring
pests & diseases	Slugs and snails may prove to become troublesome in spring on any young shoots

Woodwardia radicans

Chain fern

This magnificent fern is a most desirable garden plant, but it needs a sheltered position if it is to survive over winter, as it is rather tender. However, this luminously beautiful plant is well worth a little extra effort to keep it in good condition.

When grown in ideal conditions, *Woodwardia radicans* produces huge, arching fronds up to around 1.5m (5ft) in length, which are often bronze or red-tinted when young. These mature to a rich, glossy green, creating a waterfall of magnificent fronds.

This plant is seen to best advantage when in a slightly elevated position, perhaps on a bank. It also has the curious feature of producing plantlets from the tips of its fronds – these develop when the frond touches and remains in contact with the ground.

Snip off faded, browning fronds as the plant grows to keep it looking in good order.

To get this wonderful species to grow well, you will need to find the most sheltered corner of the garden, in a well-shaded spot with a freely draining acidic soil that is constantly moist, adding plenty of well-rotted manure when planting. The chain fern is an evergreen plant, but fronds are damaged by winter cold and the crowns will need protecting with straw and horticultural fleece.

Perhaps the simplest way to grow it is in a container, where it can be raised up with ease to show off its wonderful cascading form, and kept well watered. This way when severe winter weather strikes, the plant can spend the coldest nights inside.

Propagation is through detaching rooted plantlets from the end of the leaves, or via division of clumps in spring.

soil	Should be planted where soil is acidic, free draining and humus rich
watering	Must have constant moisture, without being waterlogged
pruning/ thinning	Very little pruning or thinning is needed, but you should remove old faded fronds if required
general care	Keep potted plants inside when first hard frosts strike. Mulch in spring with rotted manure
pests & diseases	Relatively trouble free. Pests and diseases do not usually cause any serious problems

Woodwardia radicans

Woodwardia radicans

Troubleshooting

Growing a varied range of plants in the shade attracts an equally varied selection of pests, diseases and other problems. The following diagram is designed to help you diagnose conditions suffered by your plants from the symptoms you can observe. Starting with the part of the plant that appears to be the most affected, by answering successive questions 'yes' [✓] or 'no' [✗] you will quickly arrive at a probable cause. Once you have identified the cause, turn to the relevant entry in the directory of pests and diseases for details of how to treat the problem.

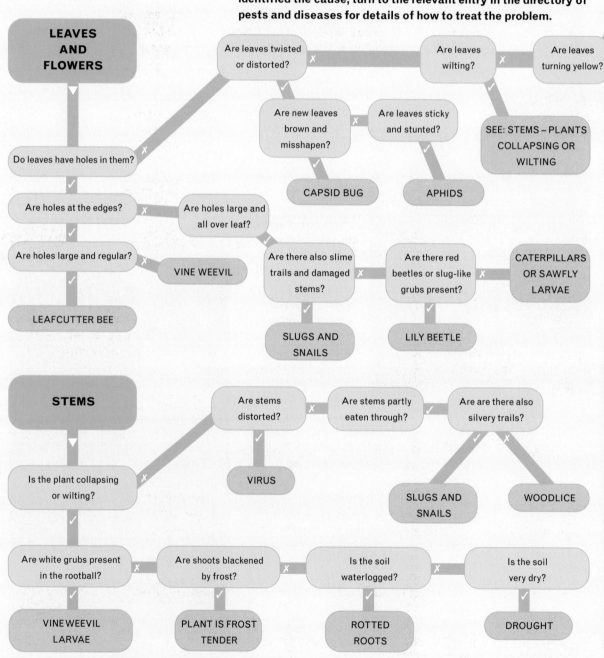

LEAVES AND FLOWERS

Are leaves twisted or distorted?
Are leaves wilting?
Are leaves turning yellow?
Are new leaves brown and misshapen?
Are leaves sticky and stunted?
SEE: STEMS – PLANTS COLLAPSING OR WILTING
Do leaves have holes in them?
CAPSID BUG
APHIDS
Are holes at the edges?
Are holes large and all over leaf?
Are holes large and regular?
VINE WEEVIL
Are there also slime trails and damaged stems?
Are there red beetles or slug-like grubs present?
CATERPILLARS OR SAWFLY LARVAE
LEAFCUTTER BEE
SLUGS AND SNAILS
LILY BEETLE

STEMS

Are stems distorted?
Are stems partly eaten through?
Are are there also silvery trails?
VIRUS
Is the plant collapsing or wilting?
SLUGS AND SNAILS
WOODLICE
Are white grubs present in the rootball?
Are shoots blackened by frost?
Is the soil waterlogged?
Is the soil very dry?
VINE WEEVIL LARVAE
PLANT IS FROST TENDER
ROTTED ROOTS
DROUGHT

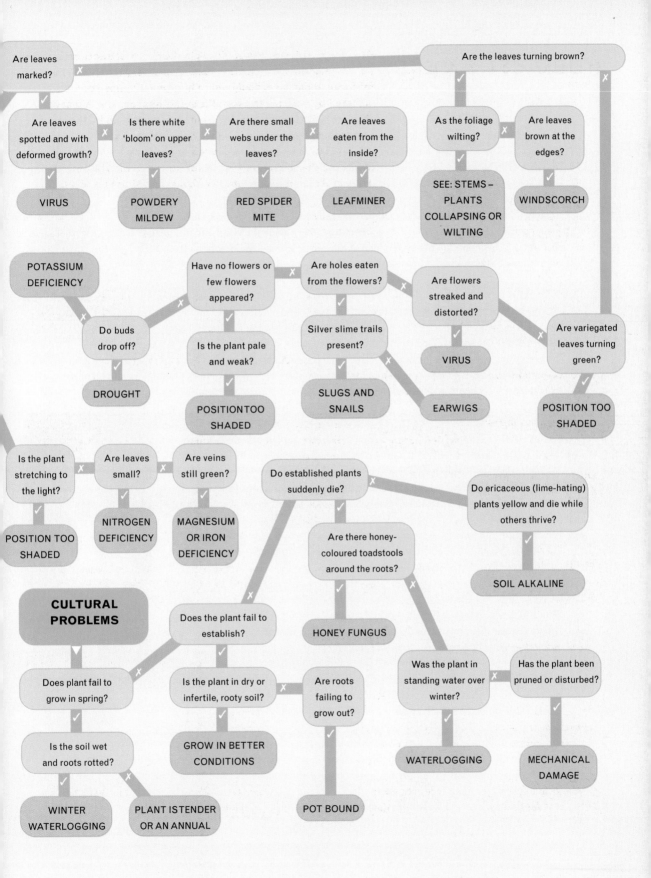

Are leaves marked?

✓

Are the leaves turning brown?

Are leaves spotted and with deformed growth? → ✗ Is there white 'bloom' on upper leaves? → ✗ Are there small webs under the leaves? → ✗ Are leaves eaten from the inside?

As the foliage wilting? → ✗ Are leaves brown at the edges?

✓ VIRUS

✓ POWDERY MILDEW

✓ RED SPIDER MITE

✓ LEAFMINER

✓ SEE: STEMS – PLANTS COLLAPSING OR WILTING

✓ WINDSCORCH

POTASSIUM DEFICIENCY

Have no flowers or few flowers appeared? → ✗ Are holes eaten from the flowers? → ✗ Are flowers streaked and distorted?

✗ Do buds drop off?

Silver slime trails present?

✓ VIRUS

Are variegated leaves turning green?

✓ Is the plant pale and weak?

✓ DROUGHT

✓ SLUGS AND SNAILS

✗ EARWIGS

✓ POSITION TOO SHADED

✓ POSITION TOO SHADED

Is the plant stretching to the light? → Are leaves small? → Are veins still green?

Do established plants suddenly die? → ✗ Do ericaceous (lime-hating) plants yellow and die while others thrive?

✓ POSITION TOO SHADED

✓ NITROGEN DEFICIENCY

✓ MAGNESIUM OR IRON DEFICIENCY

✓ Are there honey-coloured toadstools around the roots?

✓ SOIL ALKALINE

CULTURAL PROBLEMS

✗ Does the plant fail to establish?

✓ HONEY FUNGUS

Was the plant in standing water over winter? → ✗ Has the plant been pruned or disturbed?

▽

Does plant fail to grow in spring? → Is the plant in dry or infertile, rooty soil? → ✗ Are roots failing to grow out?

✓ WATERLOGGING

✓ MECHANICAL DAMAGE

✓ Is the soil wet and roots rotted?

✓ GROW IN BETTER CONDITIONS

✓ POT BOUND

✓ WINTER WATERLOGGING

✗ PLANT IS TENDER OR AN ANNUAL

Pests & Diseases
Pests

It is important to have an idea of the pests and diseases that could affect plants grown in the shade, and this short guide will give you some idea of the most common and how they can best be dealt with.

Aphids

There are many different kinds of aphid: some are known as blackfly or greenfly, but different species attack different plants. Indeed, most plants will be attacked at some time by aphids. The insects have needle like mouth parts with which they suck plant sap. Plant growth slows and new growth appears distorted and pale. The tops of leaves often become sticky as the aphids excrete honeydew. A dark, almost sooty mould often grows on this honeydew, especially in damp shade, which disfigures plants further. The aphids target the youngest growth and the aphids tend to cluster on the undersides of the leaves to feed. Minor infestations can simply be washed off, treat heavier attacks with a suitable insecticide spray.

Ants

These familiar insects seem harmless enough but can be a nuisance to gardeners. Several species are common in gardens and are most commonly seen on plants already infested with aphids, from which they collect sugary honeydew. However, it is in summer, when ants begin to build nests and later start to fly, when problems can arise. Potted plants are often used by the ants as the soil is easy for them to work, and here they can disturb plant roots and disrupt the growing plant. Lifting containers off the ground using pot 'feet' can help to prevent ant attack, but in borders and lawns, ant nests are less easy to deal with.

Vine weevil

These beetle-like black insects are among the most troublesome pests to be found in the garden. Adults will damage the foliage of many plants, such as rhododendrons, eating notches from the edges of leaves, but it is the young which cause the most damage eating away roots of many plants, especially shrubs as well as tubers of plants such as Cyclamen, eventually causing the plant to wilt, collapse and die. Adults feed mostly at night mostly in spring and summer and can lay many hundreds of eggs, the young grubs, white and legless cause most damage between autumn and late spring. Potted plants are most at risk from attack. Insecticides are available to treat plants.

Leaf miners

There are a wide range of insects that leaf mine, most of which are larvae of moths, flies or beetles. The insect eats out the inside of the leaf between the upper and lower surfaces. In shaded situations, holly (Ilex) is commonly affected, but many other species may be damaged. The damaged parts of the leaves quickly dry and turn white or brownish, the foliage of effected plants displaying twisting lines, blotches or patches, depending on the insect. These creatures are hard to control with insecticides, but although unsightly, the damage is not usually a problem.

Earwigs

Easily recognized with their long bodies ending in pairs of pincers, these creatures can damage foliage and flowers of many plants. They eat holes in petals and leaves, emerging only after dark to feed. During the day they hide amid the foliage or in dark, cool places. Look for earwigs at night by torchlight, picking off individuals, or try to trap them placing a small flowerpot full of straw upside down on the end of a cane, at about the same level as the tops of the plants.

Leafcutter bees

These remarkable insects are seldom actually seen, but their damage is often apparent. A variety of plants are affected, such as roses and epimediums. The bees, which look rather like honeybees, are solitary and the females use pieces of leaf to construct their nests. These nests are often built in compost-filled flower pots or even just in soil. Plant leaves have regularly-shaped missing pieces, but seldom cause lasting damage to the plant, unless the plant is very small. The bees return many times to the same plant to collect nest-building material.

Caterpillars and sawfly larvae

Caterpillars, the larval stage of butterflies and moths, are common pests in the garden and can cause substantial damage by eating holes in leaves or stems (*see also* leaf miners). Sawflies, related to bees and wasps, have caterpillar-like larvae, many of which can cause extensive damage to a range of plants. One of the most common, especially in shade, is Solomon's Seal Sawfly. The larvae of this species are grey and hatch out from eggs laid by the adult fly in late spring, usually as the plant begins to flower. When young they are quite small and easily missed but as they feed, they completely defoliate plants, leaving only stems by late summer. The best control is to remove the larva by hand or spray with a suitable insecticide. Plants usually recover the following year.

Lily beetle

These appealing-looking bright scarlet beetles can totally destroy the shoots and flowers of lilies and related plants, such as Fritillaria. They appear in early spring and quickly start eating holes in foliage, buds and stems of affected clumps. In summer, the larval stage appears on the leaves. The grubs look like small, sticky rounded slugs. These creatures can be found for most of the growing season and gardeners must be vigilant if they wish to grow those plants affected in areas where lily beetle is a problem. Pick off and kill the creatures, although this can be tricky with the adults, as they drop off plants if disturbed or hide under the leaves.

Diseases

Cultural problems

A wide range of cultural problems can affect plants in the garden. Frost damage, drought, waterlogging, feeding requirements, soil pH and initial planting are all examples. Healthy plants not only look more attractive, but they are also less prone to disease. A stressed plant is unlikely to survive for long. Cultural problems should always be suspected if a new or young plant fails shortly after planting, established plants are more likely to succumb to pests or disease.

Powdery mildew

An unsightly and damaging fungal disease affecting the foliage of many plants. Upper leaf surfaces are damaged first, a white bloom developing, and leaves beginning to yellow and young growth becoming distorted. In severe cases die back occurs and leaves fall early. Various fungi are responsible and are generally host specific. They are particularly prevalent in humid, shaded areas on stressed plants, especially those in dry soil. Infected leaves may be removed and fungicide sprays are available.

Honey fungus

One of the most damaging problems, honey fungus attacks trees, shrubs and climbers, even when mature. Affected plants begin to decline in health, dying back over several years for no obvious reason. Sometimes resin oozes from the stems of infected plants. The fungus spreads through the soil via root-like growth that punctures the stems and roots of plants and feed from them, eventually killing them. The most obvious sign are clumps of honey coloured toadstools near affected plants. Remove infected tree stumps and roots.

Index

Acknowledgements

The publishers would like to thank Coolings Nurseries for their cooperation and assistance with the photography in this book, including the loan of tools and much specialist equipment. Special thanks go to: Sandra Gratwick. Coolings Nurseries Ltd., Rushmore Hill, Knockholt, Kent, TN14 7NN. Tel: 00 44 1959 532269; Email: coolings@coolings.co.uk; Website: www.coolings.co.uk.